MW00942810

Chronology of Love
Times and Seasons

Keat Wade

PRESS

Frontispiece

BIRTH OF THE SPIRITED PEN

Restless spirit of little understanding
seeking to emerge through the mind and hand,
lay near dormancy within the breast,
on the edge of my imagination,
conceived, slowly growing, but never emerging.

Occasional winds of the creative fanned
the infant ember
within the soul of the restless, throbbing heart
as ideas, words, and phrases swirled
in wispy circles, yet remaining unformed
unripened or ready for harvest.

In the season of His choosing,
tendered by Holy Spirit within
reaching out through the shell of the
weakening chrysalis*
true gifts emerge as wispy circles

clear and focused into their destiny.
Such was experienced by a now humbled writer
shakily reaches out to grasp
the shimmering Excalibur ** of the printed page,
now redeemed,
dancing voyages across a white sea, settling
into the rhythmic patterns flowing through it.

Conceived and carried long within
the darkness of a soul, now set free,
by submitting the restless heart
into the hand of the Creator
that it might become the instrument of these words.

May the words flow forever
on ancient parchment of reader's minds,
remembered not
by the writer, but the author
who released it to accomplish His purposes
and allow me to Honor Him through. . .
My SpiritedPen

(Keat Wade 08/03/02)
* the hard-shelled pupa of a butterfly
** the sword drawn from the store by King Arthur

Dedication

The author claims no credit for the power of
the tender words, thoughts, or reflections expressed
between the covers of this book. They are, indeed,
a chronology of His Love for His people, all of us.
The poetic writings here are now dedicated back
to God, the one who entrusted them to His grateful
scribe. With humble thanks for the privilege of
being called to be a part of the process of sharing
His thoughts and directions for those who read and
receive, I dedicate this volume to Adonai, God of
the Angel Armies.

Acknowledgements

T he book sounded like a good idea and I loved
the thought of sharing what the Lord has given
me but I realize that it never would have happened
without the consistent encouragement of my wife,
Judy, and the persistence from the same during the
push for excellence in the bringing it all together.
With Judy, I must thank Winifred Garlow, mother of
Judy and proof-reader par-excellence, for her dili-
gence and support.

I must acknowledge, also, the many in my life,
early and late, that fed into my life-experiences, as
with any author, that become a part of the essence
of our lives. They all lend expression to what comes
from our SpiritedPen, the iconic name given to the
writing for both Judy and me.

Thanks to those who are a part of Uniting Our
Hearts in Prayer, and others who clung to God's
words and encouraged me to keep listening and
writing.

I would be in great remiss if I did not thank God as he taught me to wait on Him. It was a pathway to intimacy that opened the floodgates for His downloads gladly received at my computer keyboard in late night and early morning hours as He shared and I wrote.

FORWARD

First of all, I love poetry. I consider poetry an intersection of the prophetic gift with a psalmitry expression. When I was reading Keat Wade's book, Chronology of Love, I thought of three things: God, the Psalms of David, and my wife.

My wife Pam is a master gardener. For years she prepared herself to create gardens. This began when we were in college at Texas A&M University in College Station. We had little money, so our hobby was plants. To help me finish my education, she went to work in the Horticulture Department.

This set her on a life journey. She has sacrificed both time, sweat, and tears to reach the point where she can produce masterpieces of plants, earth, rock, and water. This year, Pam has undertaken the "green" project of her life. She has led a team of workers to create what we call The Israel Prayer Garden at the Global Spheres Center.

What an incredible place this garden is! From the moment people take their first step into the garden they enter an atmosphere like few I know. Sights, sounds, smells, tastes, and touches all come together in this garden. Above all else the garden is more a place to experience rather than a place to explain. Pam's workers have posted attractive but simple signs to explain the various parts of the garden and the anointing released in each section. Though the signs are helpful in identifying the anointing, one must walk through the garden to experience the anointing.

Keat Wade is a Master Gardener of a different kind. His tools are words and expressions; his soul (and the souls of his readers) is the soil he cultivates. Chronology of Love: Times and Season is Keat's masterpiece garden. The signs he has posted throughout this work reveal the personal and spiritual path that God has developed in Keat. They point the reader towards the anointing they can expect to encounter as they wind their way through the pathways of his work. Chronology of Love is more than a book of poems to understand. Chronology of Love is a place where your soul and your senses can experience the goodness and fullness of the Lord God—creation's Master Gardener.

The Spirit of God will touch you as you make your way through this book. He has breathed life into Keat's garden. Rather than rush your way through each page, let the Spirit breath into you poem by poem. Expect to taste things that will satisfy and new things that have never touched your soul's palate. If your day is hot then you will find a shady spot to rest. If things in your life stink then you will catch the fragrance that heals and replenishes. When you come across something you can sink your teeth into, don't be reluctant to take a big bite and let the juice run down your chin!

When God placed the first man into His Garden, He activated Adam's experience of it by commanding him to eat the garden's fruit. Once again God has created a garden through Keat Wade and has placed you in it. Experience the garden of the goodness of God.

Charles D. "Chuck" Pierce
President, Global Spheres Center
President, Glory of Zion International, Inc.

Introduction

There is a form of expression that only comes through the medium of poetry which is meant to be heard as well as read. Hearing the sound of prophetic poetry in your spirit is a way by which we can receive that which God inspires. I had dabbled in trying to create a meaningful form via the expression of poetry but had little success until . . . I met Judy, when the Lord thrust me forward into the "new". I began to experience a change that was to affect every area of my life, especially my relationship with the heavenly Father. The unfolding narrative of the chronology contains a unique story that the discerning reader will see and want to share. This is my purpose in sharing this story.

Contents

Frontispiece v
Dedication vii
Acknowledgments.. ix
Forward by Charles D. Pierce xi
Introduction xv

A Chronology of Love

In Anticipation	01/07/99	27
Majesty On the Mountain	08/22/99	29
Your Living Word	08/24/99	32
Love Worth Living	10/12/99	33
Safe Harbor	11/24/99	34
By His Light	01/01/01	36
Circles	01/01/01	38
Pressing On	01/21/01	38
Ode to My Sandcastle	09/10/01	39
The Light of His Countenance	11/28/01	41
Breath of God – Breath of Life	01/11/02	43
Praise . . .	01/24/02	46

Love Banner	03/26/02	47
Once Upon a Century	03/28/02	49
Increase My Desire	03/31/02	51
Pegs for the Lord	04/11/02	53
Worship, the Mantle of His Glory	05/10/02	54
Voice of the Shofar	05/17/02	55
Upon This Mountain	06/01/02	57
When I Choose The Proper Time	07/16/02	59
His Voice	07/21/02	60
Submission In the Shadow of His Hand	07/21/02	61
Birth of the SpiritedPen	08/03/02	62
On My Heart, Lord	08/24/02	64
The Power	08/24/02	66
Seasons of Remembrance	08/24/02	68
Spiritual Presidios	08/25/02	70
Flowing Into His River	08/29/02	72
Forever	09/10/02	74
The Cloud and the Glory	10/04/02	77
Watch for the Fire	11/19/02	79
The Master Pilot's Call	12/01/02	80
What Have I to Fear	01/01/03	84
Watch and See	01/14/03	86
Provision	01/21/03	88
Wonder of Wonders	01/25/03	89
Do You Hear It a Rumblin'	01/26/03	91
Harp and Bowl - Heaven and Earth Connectors	01/26/03	93
His Name	01/26/03	94
He Gave Me a Golden Scepter	01/27/03	97
The Spirit of Interfaith	02/03/03	98
Lighthouses and Foghorns	02/04/03	100

Its Time Has Come	04/01/03	102
Where the Spirit Flows	04/12/03	104
The Wilderness of His Love	07/11/03	106
The House Within	07/13/03	107
On Wings of Eagles	08/06/03	109
It Is Coming	01/27/04	110
Hope Deferred	02/03/04	112
Read the Wind	03/07/04	113
I Am the Land	03/14/04	114
And the Waters Shall Flow	03/21/04	115
Can You Hear Our Mountain Sing	03/27/04	117
Out of the Cave	03/27/04	119
Wings of the Dawn	04/01/04	121
In This Place	10/10/04	123
In the Golden Glow of His Glory	10/24/04	124
Symphony from His Heart	11/03/04	125
The Breaking of the Dawn	11/21/04	126
Eternal Glimpses	01/13/05	127
My Praise, They Shall Declare	02/08/05	128
Wilderness Unto Wilderness	02/08/05	129
If This Land Could Speak	02/17/05	131
The Wonder of Bonnie Brae	03/10/05	133
It Happens At the Cross	03/27/05	135
And It Shall Cover the Earth	05/01/05	136
Little Girl Within	05/03/05	137
Overwhelmed	05/12/05	139
The Power of Silence	06/12/05	141
The Silence	07/02/05	142
The New Sound	07/27/05	143
He Is Our Peace	08/10/05	144
Be Still	08/15/05	146

Quakes, Shakes and Other Phenomenon	09/09/05	147
Across the Fire	09/20/05	148
Awash With His Sound	09/23/05	150
Behold the Days	10/21/05	152
Mute Before the Throne	11/16/05	153
Within the Depths	11/21/05	155
Becoming the Now	01/20/06	156
He Cometh	01/30/06	157
Walk of Love	02/13/06	158
As the Sound of Many Waters	03/25/06	160
Go For the Gold	04/01/06	161
Faithful Housewives	04/05/06	162
Acknowledged By Him	04/12/06	163
On the Wings of Your Wind	09/17/06	164
Like No Other	08/12/07	165
Walking Words	08/14/07	166
When Silence Thunders	11/08/07	167
Vision from Michelangelo	12/08/07	168
Walk In His Light	03/15/08	170
A Word Fitly Spoken	10/06/08	171
When Life is Full	01/30/09	173
Inverted Hourglass	02/27/09	175
In the Spray of the Fountain	04/22/10	177
Cross Over, Now	04/23/10	178
Softly Beating Heart	04/29/10	179
Red, Runs the Rio	05/01/10	181
Voices	05/02/10	183
Is That You, God?	05/25/10	184
When Worlds Collide	07/30/10	186
Fountain Covenant	08/01/10	187
Cascading Waterfalls	08/01/10	190

Bombshell   08/16/10 191
Wind and Fire   08/27/10 193
The Black Hole of Despair   10/12/10 194
Walk the Path Alone   10/17/10 195
The Faith Whisperer   10/30/10 196
The Dawning of a New Day   11/01/10 197
Softly the SOUND That
THUNDERS   11/08/10 199
The Power of Alignment   11/08/10 201
Be Still and Know That I AM . . .
Will   11/09/10 202
MARCH   11/12/10 203
Our Hearing Hearts   11/19/10 205
Time Traveler – Then and Now   11/26/10 206
Three Angel Poems   12/04/10 207
From the Courtroom of Heaven   12/09/10 209
Bushes and Bulrushes   12/27/10 210
Shabbat Shalom   01/07/11 211
Oh, Little Town of Escondido   01/08/11 212
Enter Intercession California   01/16/11 213
Beasts and Angels   01/20/11 215
Cherishing the Secret Place   01/23/11 216
Chosen and Prepared   02/08/11 218

Afterword

Bushes and Bulrushes   12/27/10 219

Appendix   Alphabetical List of Poems 221

A Chronology of Love

With no hint of the newness of life and experience that lay before me after experiencing tragedy, loss, and grief in my family, my expectancy for the future was not bright. Then, I began to experience the throes of change. What unfolded was a series of events that could only have been orchestrated by the Father Himself.

After losing my wife to cancer in 1996 and a two and a half year old grandson less than a year later, I traveled from Kansas in late January 1999, where I lived, to deliver a trailer load of restored oak antique office furniture for a friend in Los Angeles, California. It became a strange new experience, one of many new experiences to come. Earlier, on January first I had met a lady named Judy and began a new e-mail relationship. She lived in San Diego, California. As long as I was to be in California we agreed that I should spend some time in San Diego after the delivery of the furniture. With arrangements to stay with newfound friends, I stayed a month. We spent much of the daytime working together and did special things in the evenings, making each one special.

We made some well thought-out decisions, though very rapidly. Result: I returned to my home in Kansas, finished another project in my wood-shop, closed my business and home, loaded my pickup and trailer and headed back to California. Judy and I were married near the end of March.

In this process, my relationship with Jesus became more intense and personal. The capacity to listen and hear in my spirit opened new doors of opportunity and expression.

Chronology of Love is a collection of poetic expression over a 12 year period, 1999-2011. A developing process of moving into His presence allowed Him to download the many writings that were to follow. The words often came in the early hours of the morning from 2 to 4 a.m. The words would come as I sat at the computer and wrote what I heard in my spirit. Although some were prose words of enlightenment and encouragement, most came in the form of prophetic poetry. Many times the words just came as if through a conduit and I simply keyboarded them onto the screen. At other times the Lord seemed to be sitting beside me and we were just having fun writing . . . together.

The reader will also see a story flow through the chronology of these writings, as I have. It is a story of progression and growth in life experiences, life learning, and an increase in levels of relationship with the Lord. The poems will reflect the growing capacity for experiencing His presence.

May you experience the fullness of the journey in this upward spiral into heavenly realms. Let these words take you on a timeless journey.

1999

In Anticipation -After meeting Judy on New Year's weekend, 1999 we arranged to meet again in San Diego, where she lived. I did not consider myself a poet. However, after I met Judy, that changed. I began to write and send poetry to her. Then thinking of my former experiences at beaches and knowing that we would be spending time at the ocean, the poetic experience came to full expression in the following poem. It became a turning point in our relationship.

In Anticipation

The sound of the surf
and gulls in the sky
we create new memories
as hand in hand we fly.

With the sand beneath our feet
and the sea breeze in our hair,
we share more of our lives
making days ever fair.

As we look in the distance at
vanishing line of sea and sand,
they disappear together while
ever subtly reshaping the land.

With you by my side
the beach stretching on,

you like the sea,
me like the land,
. . .life reshapes as I move along.

Whatever may come,
wherever I go,
with you by my side
it is bound to surpass
. . .any good thing I know.

(Keat Wade 01/07/99)

Majesty On the Mountain
Story of Development

This writing was inspired by the many events, difficulties, prophetic occurrences, bureaucratic maze, agency blockages that occurred during the site development and construction of the first building in a planned church campus. There was a literal pillar of fire, the forced bridging of a dry stream bed, encountering blue granite (the hardest of its kind) which puts the church on the Solid Rock, literally and figuratively, Black-tailed Gnat Catchers and other annoyances ad infinitum all contributed to endless delays and enormous over-expenditure of time and funds. But God is good and his people, obedient and persistent. On the rough concrete walls behind the neatly finished interior walls are scriptures and prayers written by members of the doggedly persistent believers from children just beginning to write to older members mobile enough to preserve the Word for eternity. Scriptures were prayed all across the property and throughout the building during the entire period of construction even during the clean up and move-in completed during the final hours before the first service on Psalm Sunday, 2000.

It is important to understand all of this to get the full impact of the poem and the prophetic phrases within it. As His words flowed through me onto the computer screen before me, I was amazed and in awe knowing what He had accomplished in spite of all the obstacles. The parenthetical scriptural inclusions represent key words prayed during the completion of the project.

Majesty On the Mountain

When all the paperwork is done,
After the technical battles won,
The healing waters shall flow
(John 14:4)
And there will be Majesty on the Mountain.
(Is 2:2-3)

The scriptures hidden in the walls
(Ps 119:161; Ps 119:25)
Will flow as sparkling water falls
(John 7:38-39)
As they continue to speak
From the Majesty on the Mountain.

When the last steel has been set in place,
And the Throne room is given space,
(Ps 89:4)

The Word of God shall be proclaimed
(Ps 107:20)
From the Majesty on the Mountain.

The fire of God shall roar
(Zech 2:5)
The healing waters pour
(Is 44:3)

O'er the land of restoration from the one
(Ps 85:1)
Who inhabits the Majesty on the Mountain.
All God's people shall be blessed
As they enter into His rest
And worship Him forever
From the Majesty on the Mountain.

The roar of Judah's Lion
Gentleness from the Lamb of Zion,
The shadow of the Cross of Christ,
Embody... the Majesty on the Mountain.

Renewed for the battle for the souls of men
We shall go forth to serve amid the din
In a spirit of sacrificial love
From the Majesty on the Mountain.

Forged by His Presence
(Zech 4:6-7)
Filled by His Essence,
(Ps 85:9)
Truth and righteousness will flow
(Ps 89:9; Ps 85:11, 13)
From the Majesty on the Mountain.

Inhabiting the Majesty on the Mountain,
... HE IS the Majesty on the Mountain.

(Keat Wade 08/22/99)

Your Living Word

You, Oh God are light, the Light
which is a lamp unto my feet,
illuminating my pathway as it leads me
to the place that is higher than I
which you have prepared for me
where I can dwell in your house, Oh Lord, forever.

Though I may go through many valleys
You will lift me to soar to lofty peaks
where I can see the lighted way
that you have prepared for those who love You.

When the battles are over and won
and the valleys are washed clean
with the pure, flowing water from holy peaks,
then we shall all dwell in that peace
that passes all understanding,
As we rest in Your Presence, eternally.

(Keat Wade 08/24/1999)

Love Worth Living

Love comes in many forms and in many ways
making life worth loving...Love is worth living.

First God loved me and patiently waited for me
to recognize my need for Him...Love was worth
living.

He continued to provide molding opportunities
through life experience...making Love worth living.

He continues to lift me to higher planes of learning
and feeling His great love...sealing Love worth
living.

He brought new light and new love into my life
through Judy
When He blended our lives...acknowledging Love is
worth sharing...

Now, we three, move in new planes of the light of
his Love
as He reveals clarity on the other side of the glass
seen darkly,
but then clearly...as he makes Love the fulfillment
of living.

(Keat Wade 10/12/99)

Safe Harbor

How we glory in you, Oh, Lord.
You are the precious cord
that binds us to all that
You have for us...
in Your safe Harbor.

No matter how high the winds
Your breakwater will always defend
those whom we hold dear
on the placid water...
of Your safe harbor.

From the enemy's windy gust
surrounding shores protect us.
Seeking sanctuary from the quest,
finding solitude and peaceful rest...
in the safety of Your harbor.

Under attack, but always blest;
riding the storms, we face the test,
knowing when its done, we shall rest
and in the peaceful waters, trust...
anointed by waters of Your safe harbor.

When the winter gales pass
spring will follow and, alas,
we shall row ashore and step at last
into the healing waters on the beach so vast

and rest forevermore on the shores of...
Your Safe Harbor.

(Keat Wade, 11/24/99)

2001

By His Light

The truth of His Word
is seen clearly.

The enemy flees
fearing being exposed.

Hearts are warmed
for it is more than light.

Heavy to the rebellious
buoyant to the obediently compliant.

Faltering hearts
are strangely lifted to His.

Closed ears
are opened to His Voice.

Narrowed pupils
dilate wide.

Empty souls
are filled.

Closed gates
are opened.

Hell shunned,
Heaven entered.

(Keat Wade 01/01/01)

Circles

To live is to love.
To love is to learn.
To learn is to grow wise.
To be wise is to share.
To share is to live…
Let the circle continue.

(Keat Wade, 01/01/01)

Pressing On

Hand in hand we span time and space
as we enter a new prophetic day.
While being equipped for the race,
unanticipated gifts come our way.

Growing in discernment and wisdom
we seek to speak truth and peace
as we walk in the realm of His Kingdom
and in His Spirit, find release.

Many darts and arrows come our way
but we boldly divert them with His righteous shield.
We live and work confidently day by day
as we plow deep furrows in His fertile field.

(Keat Wade, 01/21/01)

Ode to My Sand Castle - Composed for Sharon and Curt Davis, Sept. 10, 2001
In appreciation for all that they do to enhance the lives of others. The "Sand Castle" was the home of Sharon's friend where she spent parts of many childhood summers. Now, as owners, Sharon and Curt have made it a wonderful retreat.

Ode to My Sand Castle

Quaint but magnificent,
crowded but isolated,
an ethereal dream, now a reality
is My Sand Castle

The playground of my childhood,
my refuge by the sea,
now an anointed retreat
is My Sand Castle.

Near sand and surf
where hearts and imagination may soar
and be filled through God's blessing,
is My Sand Castle.

The dream from my childhood
fulfilled in adulthood
by My Heavenly Father
is My Sand Castle.

May all who inhabit
however short or long
be blessed by His Presence
in My Sand Castle.

(Keat Wade 09/10/01)

The Light of His Countenance

When the world seems dark
and the shadows are deep:
though the walls tower o're us
we can walk the unknown
in the light of His countenance.

Buildings can come down
while threatening with fear
through the deeds of evil.
Yet we fearlessly follow His map
by the light of His countenance.

The tide is turning; we will prevail
as we move reclaiming territory
claimed by he who fell from grace;
who roared threateningly, but now must retreat
under the light of His countenance.

Intercessors are arising, uniting
while the tsunami of youth is bulging upward
drawing all streams of believers into the strong
currents
all coming together in powerful overcoming
strength
fully empowered by the light of His countenance.

His church, the body of Christ shall prevail
filled by the power of His love
engulfing the earth,
covering it with

the light of His countenance.
(Keat Wade, 11/28/01)

The Light of His Countenance - This poem was later selected by Chuck Pierce for inclusion in his book *Worship Warrior*, in the chapter titled Portals of Glory.

2002

Breath of God – Breath of Life

The earth was formless, empty, and dark.
Then, He spoke the light into being,
dispelling the darkness
and it was good.

He spoke and light and darkness were separated.
Night and Day came through his voice
allowing for evening and morning
ending the first day.

God spoke the expanse into existence
forming the dry land dividing the seas.
And God said that it was good.
Ending the second day.

Then, He called forth vegetation
that would seed the land and bear fruit,
all their own kind,
all between morning and evening the third day.

He spoke the stars to spangle the night sky
to mark the seasons and days and years.
Giving light to the earth came the sun by day
and the moon by night, ending the fourth day.

At His word waters teemed with living creatures,
birds filled the expanse of the sky

at the command of His voice and
it was good in His sight at the end of the fifth day.

The land produced living creatures,
both livestock and wild creatures
and God saw that it was good,
almost complete.

Then God intimately created man
molded by His hands, rather than speaking,
breathing into him the breath of Life
giving him a living soul in the image of
a living God, unique in all His creation
with blessing and dominion over all that He had
done.

. . .And it was good.

(Keat Wade 01/11/02)

Breath of God-Breath of Life - In the poem "Breath of God – Breath of Life," the word spangle" is used in the stanza "He spoke the stars to spangle the night sky." The word spangle comes from an old classic poem. "And God waved his arm and spangled the skies with the stars" referred to that part of God's creative work taken from a poem "The Creation", in which early African-American writer, James Weldon Johnson wrote and spoke in the cadence of black preachers of his time.

After one year of teaching on a temporary certificate, I did student teaching in speech and English to fulfill requirements for a standard teaching certificate in Kansas. I had one high school remedial English student and two advanced high school sophomore English students. The remedial student and I had a common interest in poetry. Taking advantage of his fascination with "The Creation," I developed an interpretive reading project for presentation to an audience of two. As a new fan of James Weldon Johnson's poetry, I learned a great deal also, along with the two sophomore students who became the presenters fan club as well.

Praise...

Exalts Your name
above all others
renews Your claim
upon us, Your brothers.

Praise...
lifts Your name on high
letting our spirits soar
as our hearts to You draw nigh
to You through the opened door.

Worship...
our highest form of praise
as we shout and lift our voice
inspiring new songs raised
to flow in Your Presence, our choice.

We desire only You
coming into our midst
saturating us as the morning dew
equipping us for service, highly blest.

(Keat Wade 01/24/02)

Love Banner – During this period of time in which this was written, we learned much about banners, flags and streamers as a part of worship. Much of our understanding came from worshiping with Klee Adonai and particularly from Roberta. Judy and Mary Anderson were asked to be a part of Roberta's wedding. On the platform they unfolded the purple banner, spread it and began wafting the banner in rhythm to the music
"Ode to Joy," by Beethoven, creating a Chuppa-like atmosphere representing the covering of Holy Spirit for the Bride and Groom.

Love Banner

"...And His banner over me was love." Song 2:4

His banner billows over us
light filament of gossamer love
pulsating with our worship
lifted on wings like a dove.

Buoyant with our worship
tenderly floating as it fills
it is our strong protection
causing our enemy to chill.

Light is His banner
great is His Love
as His banner billows over us
keeping us, from His throne above.

As He descends to the banquet hall,
He beckons us to His table
heavy laden with all the things that fill us
too rich and satisfying for label.

Hearts are deeply stirred, aware that
His banner billows upward floating softly as a dove
little flutter, rise or fall is sensed,
His banner o'er us eternally filled with love.

Come unto me,
Believe in me,
Trust in me,
Rest in me,
Find peace in me,
Let your worship rise into the air,
Continually filling my banner,
For my banner arching over you is an endless
...CANOPY of LOVE!
(Keat Wade, 03/26/02)

Once Upon a Century

New life, deeper love, wider vision
came with the dawning
of year two thousand
as we were bid, ENTER IN.

New life meant leaving behind that which we knew
to receive that new thing which He was to reveal
as we walk in the NOW of His presence
unrestricted, unbound by things of the past or future.

Free from passing fear of Y2K
and the bonds of time, in the NOW
we move steadily, confidently on
under the banner/canopy of His Love.

Free of the past, yet so undeniably tied
we are walking unbound into the future
at peace in His wake upon a sea of glass
whose depths are only known and stirred by Him.

In a new walk, in the midst of heavenly warring,
we await the strategy from the Throne of Glory,
that puts new weapons in our hands
approaching the ultimate battles to which we are
called.

Though the promises are true and the outcome known
there is much to salvage, and enemy to be crushed.
For we are His army following the strategy of our
Commander

reclaiming that which was lost that all may be restored...

...Once Upon a Century.

(Keat Wade, 03/28/02)

Increase My Desire – This was the beginning of our experiencing angels at Skyline Church. We had felt hints of their presence at our monthly Uniting Our Hearts In Prayer meetings in another location but at Skyline, Judy saw, for the first time, angel activity in the form of swirling in the atmosphere streaked with color which mirrored the increasing intensity of the worship. As she described it to me, I had a spiritual sense of what she was seeing and sensing.

Increase My Desire

The desire was there, to see the angels
that are present in the midst
of our adulation of praise
and our adoration in His worship.

Often felt but seen by few,
each secretly desirous to experience
the messenger protectors that gather
in numbers, filling the atmosphere.

As worship rises to reach the heavens
they appeared in the minds-eye of one
who experienced the mass of their
movement round and round the room.

As worship grew stronger
the swirling, whirling figures
were blurs of white, full of light
streaked with streams of colors of the dawn
surrounding a bright beam of heavenly light

centered on the spot where worship was the strongest
radiating out beyond the heavenly stream
encompassing all whose voices rose to Him.

To open ones eyes is to lose
the visual experience, yet
the image is a snapshot
in the mind that cannot be deleted.

They are there in our worship
yet, they hear the hurting heart
and are there quietly
treating the sobbing soul.

They are there joining in swirling adoration
amplifying our praise with heavenly voices
or silently present in the most painful moments
arms around us
arms lifting us
to the throne room where we can join the dance of
the angels.

(Keat Wade, 03/31/02)

Pegs for the Lord - Inspired by a small group of women drawn together by a common vision and mutual will to carry out a commission in service for God.

Pegs for the Lord

Arise O you Deborahs.
Follow close O you Baraks.
Gather your pegs O you Jaels.
Victory is in your hands.
The Lord of Israel is leading.

Listen closely O you Deborahs.
Lead the armies O you Baraks.
Lift the hammer you Jaels.
Strike as the Lord commands.
The Lord of Israel goes before us.

Obedient and wise Deborahs, speak.
Faithful and confident Baraks, lead.
Gentle but strong Jaels, act.
Driving pegs for the Lord.
Prevailing as the Lord of Israel leads His people.

>   (Keat Wade 04/11/02,
>   based on Judges 4 & 5)

Worship, the Mantle of His Glory

On the wings of worship, we rise as an eagle,
Catching the breath of God, rising even higher
Spreading wings, soaring with angels in the
heavenly realm
Soaring, rising, soaring, touching the
fringe of heaven.

A vast expanse can be seen, yet our eaglic
(eagle-like) vision
Remains centered on the familiar realms
of our launch
Giving a clear revelation of strongholds,
Their weakness now exposed and open to attack.

Holy Spirit strength filling the lofty atmosphere
Encompasses those who dare soar near Heaven's
gates.
Prepared for war, the target in sight, wings fold
As the rapid descent begins as an arrow in flight.

Strongholds fall by the power of His Spirit
Carried on the wings of worship, exploding the
black shadows
Scattering new light, eternal light from
realms of Glory
Erasing the work of the agents of darkness.
(Keat Wade 5/10/02)

The Voice of the Shofar - April 30, 2002, National Day of Prayer, San Diego County/City Administration Building located on Harbor Drive. Facing the Pacific Ocean, twelve of us stepped forward from between banners to give the shofar blasts. Fourteen days later, I wrote the poem from that experience.

The Voice of the Shofar

Ringing through the air
Echoing through valleys and canyons
The sound of renewal and inspiration
Is the Voice of the Shofar.

Resonating, mellow or intense
In long, short or staccato blasts
Near and far away the sounds swirl and flow
It's voice touching the heart of God.

Calling to battle, ritual, or worship
The sound filling the soul
Of His chosen, His body,
Is the Voice of the Shofar.

Inspiration to man
Pleasant to God
Notice of His Sovereignty
Is the Voice of the Shofar.

Enemies flee
As armies unite

Under His banner
At the sound of…
The Voice of the Shofar.
(Keat Wade 5/17/02)

Upon This Mountain

From the plain He led you
rising a niche at a time
He moves you upward, as
on His Mountain, you climb.

Always in pursuit of Him
in the habitation of His dwelling
reaching higher and higher
each step with heart swelling.

The journey began,
you never looked back.
With Don at Your side
God left nothing to lack.

Sharing this plateau with you
our pleasure has been
yet, dreading the time
when this phase would end.

So upward you climb
as the way gets steeper
and you continue to go
much higher and much deeper.

Two armies you serve;
both, your time do merit.
One Army called Salvation
One army of His Spirit.

Reaching ever upward, scaling carefully,
your steps He does guide,
but we will still meet again, perhaps,
coming around the other side.

Many paths provide footing for the sure
as we boldly, obediently follow,
unable to see the next step
as He places our feet in the next hollow.

Upward we all travel
on our paths He aligns
as we trust Him supremely
in our life He designed.

SEE YOU AT THE TOP. . .
(Keat Wade 06/01/02)

Upon This Mountain - Written in honor of Lt. Col. Deborah Bell, The Salvation Army, one who has the heart of an intercessor. Stationed in San Diego she and her husband, Lt. Col. Don Bell were being promoted and transferred to Long Beach, California.

When I Choose the Proper Time

Thankfully, fearlessly we come
As wondrous works.
Declaring Your name
For You have chosen the proper time.
Because you have chosen Me, exaltation will come,
My Kingdom will arise
Firmly set
When I choose the proper time.
Our horns will not be lifted up
With those who deal boastfully
And those who stiff-neckedly speak
For You have not chosen the time.
Exultation not
From north, east, south or west
But God is judge who puts down or lifts up
When He has chosen the time.
The red wine pours from the cup of the Lord
Its dregs bitter in the mouths of the wicked
For they will drain and drink them down
In the chosen time of the Lord.
Declare His name forever.
Sing praises to our God
For, even now,
The Horns of the wicked are cut off
While exalted are the horns of the righteous.
Look and see...For His chosen time is come.
(Keat Wade. 07/16/02 Based on Psalm 75.)

His Voice

Thoughts from Psalm 29

Do you hear it?
Quiet, listen now:
Just above the sound of
Breaking waves
And running tide,,,
His *Voice?*

Do you hear it?
In the thunder
Powerful, full of majesty
Breaking cedars
Dividing flames of fire ...
His *Voice?*

Do you hear it?
Shaking the wilderness
The wilderness of Kadesh
Causing the deer to give birth
Strippng the forest bare
While people in the temple shout "Glory"?

From His throne room
Where He sits forever
Giving strength to His people
Blessing His people with peace
He whispers, "Listen" ...
Hear the *Voice* of I AM!
(Keat Wade 07/21/02)

Submission in the Shadow of His Hand

How awesome is the enormity of our God
Whose presence enwraps the earth
reaching out to enrapture every son and daughter
whether perched on the edge of eternity
or just breathing in the first wafts of love
experienced only in the Shadow of Your hand.

When all seems lost and the enemy gloats
we surely know whence to flee.
For His arm reaches across
the baseless fears and ongoing jeers
through the clouds of our affliction
casting comforting shadows where His own may
enter.

However huge the war torn battlefield
the shadows He casts covers all
as we trust and rest in His promises
coming before Him with our praises
in an infinite spirit of worship,
submitted. . . resting In the Shadow of His Hand.
(Keat Wade 7/21/02)

Birth of the SpiritedPen

Restless spirit of little understanding
seeking to emerge through the mind and hand,
lay near dormancy within the breast,
on the edge of my imagination,
conceived, slowly growing, but never emerging.

Occasional winds of the creative fanned
the infant ember
within the soul of the restless, throbbing heart
as ideas, words, and phrases swirled
in wispy circles, yet remaining unformed,
unripened or ready for harvest.

In the season of His choosing,
tendered by a Holy Spirit within
reaching out through the shell of the
weakening chrysalis*
true gifts emerge as wispy circles
clear and focused into their destiny.

Such was experienced by a now humbled writer
shakily reaches out to grasp
the shimmering Excalibur ** of the printed
page, now redeemed,
dancing voyages across a white sea, settling
into the rhythmic patterns flowing through it.

Conceived and carried long within
the darkness of a soul, now set free,
by submitting the restless heart

into the hand of the Creator
that it might become the instrument of these words.

May the words flow forever
on ancient parchment of reader's minds,
remembered not
by the writer, but the Author
who released it to accomplish His purposes
and allow me to Honor Him through. . .
My Spirited Pen

(Keat Wade, 08/03/02

* the hard-shelled pupa of a butterfly
** the sword drawn from the store by King Arthur

Birth of the SpiritedPen -

Excalibur was very important to me in choosing a word that described what I experienced as I tried to write alone. The sword, Excalibur, was stuck in a boulder waiting for the use of the one for which it was created. It came free in my hand and became the SpiritedPen that the Lord had prepared for me.

A *chrysalis*, housing the self-encased caterpillar, is a very difficult shell for the pupa, now turned butterfly, from which to breakout, spread its wings to dry and take flight as a strong, beautiful butterfly. I felt that paralleled my struggle to develop the use of a gift for writing. The same one who created that sequence for the caterpillar was also the one who placed the gift within me that made this flow of poetry possible.

On My Heart, Lord

On my heart, Lord. Your words abide,
write no more on cold stone.
Rather on the tablets of my heart
shall your laws be written.
Let men know You
because they have known me
as they recognize Your signature
on these throbbing inscriptions
etched by Your hand
on my heart, Lord,
that forgiveness, reconciliation, restoration
may occur in our hearts
sins to be remembered no more
at the reading of these hearts.

(Keat Wade 08/24/02 Based on Jeremiah 31:33-34)

On My Heart, Lord - Jeremiah 31:33-34 – [33]But this is the covenant that I will make with the house of Israel after those days, says the Lord: I will put My law in their minds, and write it on their hearts; and I will be their God, and they shall be My people. [34]No more shall every man teach his neighbor, and every man his brother, saying, 'Know the Lord,' for they shall know Me, from the least of them to the greatest of them, says the Lord. For I will forgive their iniquity, and their sin I will remember no more."

The Power

The power of Your Word
rumbles throughout the earth
wherever released
bursting from spirit-filled hearts.

The power of Your breath
whistles through hallowed halls,
across Your chosen lands
to fill the lungs of those who shout Your glory.

Your mighty right arm
undergirds the embattled spirits
of hearts heavy in intercession
in the gaps and on the walls.

Your word causes storms to rise
and storms to cease.
At the sound of Your voice
all creation will one day come to order.

No other power
above, upon, or beneath the earth
compares nor commands
all to bow in submission.

Yours alone is the power
that possesses forever
in its natural sustaining force

that which You place in each of us
. . . the power for eternity.

(Keat Wade 08/24/02)

Seasons of Remembrance

Fresh is the season of
New life, new beginnings, newness of spirit
Birth, innocence, clean and pure.
We call it Spring.

Vibrant, undaunted, invincible,
Stands huge in the heart of our remembrance;
Subject to error of fearless impulse.
We call it Summer.
Knowledge, understanding, creeping gray
Brings hints of wisdom, strategy, thoughtful
contemplation;
Older, wiser, discerning guiding voices.
We call it Autumn.

Slower, methodical, mechanical in body.
Merciful, keenly thoughtful, living in the
abundance, blessed;
Sharing with Spring, Summer, Autumn,
seeing fulfillment.
We call it Winter.

Complete in His providence
Seeds have fallen
Nurtured in due season
Continuing the cycle...
We know them as seasons, seasons of Life.
(Keat Wade 08/24/02)

Seasons of Remembrance - As we grow in wisdom and maturity, we should be able to look back and contemplate our seasons. "And you shall remember the Lord your God, for it is He who gives you power to get wealth, that He may establish His covenant which He swore to your fathers, as it is this day." Deuteronomy 8:18

Spiritual Presidios

Before the fort,
was planted a cross
in the name of One
Who is a mighty fortress.

On a high place
a commanding view
a fortress was established,
The Presidio.

Padre Junipero Serra's
first step of establishment
of many fortresses to come
in a chain of coastal fortresses.

With the spiritual fortresses
now a shadow of the intent of their founder
we must take up the task, fortress builders
of spiritual strongholds, our presidios,
reclaiming and closing
gateways forfeited, now regained.

(Keat Wade, completed
08/25/02)

Spiritual Presidios – Any study of California history will inevitably include the name
Padre Junipero Serra. A man with a compassion for sharing his faith with the indigenous people of the land, he built the first mission church in the state and

then began a lifetime of building a series of missions up the Pacific coast from San Diego to Sonoma. The path he followed is now called El Camino Real, "the royal highway." We have learned to greatly appreciate the work of this singularly focused man of God and the heritage he left behind. This writing reflects our appreciation of his work.

Flowing Into His River

From the high places
To the midlands
To the low places
We gravitate into the waters
Flowing toward the sea
Forming streams, mingling souls
Ever joining in union
Becoming a single stream merging,
growing, swelling
Coursing into the River of God

As the growing, moving waters
Ever change the face of the land
So our streams grow
In volume, power, authority
Impacting, cleansing
Carrying away impure sediment
To be dumped into
The seas of no remembrance
To be heard of no more
Carried by His purifying River.

The barest trickle
Of His tiniest rivulets
Flows to Him
Ever merging, ever growing
Streams increasing in strength

Gaining authority over the land
In and ever growing body, enmeshing

Into His binding, engulfing love
Molding a natural force
Into a powerful River of God.

Self-seeking gone
Wills merged
Commitment confirmed
Coming together, dedicated
To His planned course
Created to move ever in Him
In one body, growing in purity
Fulfilling our covenant
Receiving Him
In his river of love.
(Keat Wade 08/29/02)

Forever

Thoughts from Psalm 23

I have a shepherd
Whose name I know,
He keeps me
Where no want is known.

Down I lie in rest, at His command
In His sanctuary of green pastures
Along the intimate paths, He leads
Near peaceful still waters.
There I find restoration
For my soul
As I follow
Without reservation.

He takes me on His path
Of peace, called Righteousness.
Nothing to fear
Only the Lord and me.

I am His child
A part of His family;

He does this for me
For His names sake.

Wherever He leads
I walk securely

Even under the shadow
Of death itself.

No fear of evil
Is there for me
For beside me
Is my Father, my Friend.

I am comforted
Under the Shepherd's hands
Wielding a rod of defense
And a guiding staff.

A table He prepares
As our enemies stand harmlessly by
And the oil of His anointing
Flows over my head.

The cup of supply
Fills quickly
Overflowing
With plenty.

As our shared path grows longer
It is filled with His goodness
And assuring mercy.
All my days shall be so ordered, forever.

I have found my dwelling place
Both for here, for NOW, and by invitation
Into His house
To continually abide, forever

And FOREVER,
and forever
and forever and forever and forever and forever...

(Keat Wade 09/10/02)

The Cloud and the Glory

Cloud our tabernacle that your Glory may fill it.
Let us rest and bask in You until
You give the command to move
as Your Cloud of Glory lifts and leads us on.

We know by the movement
of Your Cloud of Glory
Your desire for us
to move forward in You.

Marked by Your Cloud of Glory
during restful communion by day
and nighttime pillars of fire
we exist in You alone.

Let us falter not in our following
as did your children of ancient historical days
that we may not only rest under
Your cloud, but receive Your Glory.

Following Your Glory Cloud by day
safe behind Your pillar of fire by night
we move forward,
our confidence ever in You.

As Glory Clouds engulf us, we rest.
As they lift, we follow
safe in the arms
of love of our heavenly Father.

The spirit of Your tabernacle abides with us
as clouds of glory surround us
for we are tabernacles of meeting where
we commune with you.

Your presence is what we desire
entering the tabernacle
worshipping, praising, seeking
intimacy with You.
(Keat Wade 10/04/02)

Watch for the Fire

Watch for the fire, His miracle fire
at unexpected moments
in unusual times
for His anointed purposes.

To protect from the brilliance
of His face
Moses only heard Your voice
from a burning bush.

Enemies from Egypt were held at bay
by a pillar of fire
that was the <u>rearguard</u>
for Your children, released to return home.

Three were thrown in
but four were seen in the white hot furnace,
soon to step out untouched, unscorched,
by the enemie's all consuming fires.

When flames leap high and all seems lost,
I will not flee but look for You
in the midst of the fire for Your protection
to show forth Your blazing Glory.
(Keat Wade, 11/19/02)

The Master Pilot's Call

The River of Life must be
navigated with purpose.
Awareness of the obstacles
allows us to steer around them
finding the best channel
through the rapids.

Too long, I drifted,
the tiller unmanned
being caught in the worst
of the rapids
often trapped in the backwaters
swirling eddies of going nowhere.

Somehow released without warning
I went spinning downstream
only to be caught time after time
in the logjams and shallows
of life without a pilot
and no river charts.

I was pinned again,
this time above a fork
between the swamp of despair
and the stream of final disaster
as a voice penetrated my darkness
from a strangely inviting campfire on the shore.

"I can help you if you call."
"What can you do?

The logs are too tangled
for anyone to free me.
You are only one."
"Just call me," is all He said.

Helpless with fading hope
my trembling lips uttered, "Come."
Without hesitation
or even looking down,
across the logs he came,
no lumberjack could rival.
As His voice and His presence
soothed my soul
His hand covered mine
on the tiller of my ship.
Soon we found open water
where carpenter hands began repairs.
Under gentle prodding
and His wise counsel
we began to work
against the current
steering carefully,
objects of evil force now seen.

My new pilot seemed to know
the dangers around each bend
as we worked clear, one by one.
"Now we can get back into the flow."
"NO, we will find a better way,
a way back, unloading bad cargo taken on."

I began to understand
as we entered the channel of repentance
crossing pools of reconciliation
that brought changes in my ship,
repairs taking place that seemed impossible
except for the outstretched hand of my pilot.

We reached the headwaters of my life stream
feeling clean, refreshed, restored.
"If I can stand beside you at the tiller
we will find the true channel in your river."
Trembling, my hand came off the tiller,
allowing His to take it's place.

The river looked different now.
The darkness and foreboding
of objects ahead, avoided by
a new sense of discernment and destiny
as I stood firm on the deck
hand firmly clasped by a Master Pilot.
With purpose and trust
we now navigate new waters.
Still fraught with danger
yet avoided by discernment,
strength, and clear vision
through submission to my pilot, called Jesus.

The journey is not finished
with unknown miles to go,
yet I sail on, now watchful
for those haplessly drifting

toward wide mouthed inviting entries
into branches of destruction.

Perhaps they will hear my call,
"I have a pilot who knows the way
through treacherous waters.
Come, sail with us and learn of Him
and we will dock in His safe harbor
at the end of the journey, together."

HEED THE CALL.......
(Keat Wade 12/01/02)

2003

What Have I to Fear?

When life becomes unbearable
And filled with treacherous terrain
Convinced that I am culpable,
Filled with fear and worthy of disdain,
I have One who promises to go before
While a rear guard He will be, What have I to fear?

When comes the torrential rains,
I am under His umbrella.
Do I have ought to fear?

When the path seems impassible,
His vehicle is all-terrain.
Where comes the fear?

When the fires become too intense to bear
His insulation of love keeps me from singe and
smoke.
Meshech knew
Shadrach knew
Abednego knew[1]
Why should I fear?

My Shield, my Defender, my Protector, my Savior,
The One who promised to go before me,
The same promises to be a rear guard.
None is greater, the Lord Sabaoth,

The Lord of Hosts reigns,
What have I to fear?
(Keat Wade 01/01/03)

Watch and See

Watch in 2003
a time to see
in 2002 you were to wait.
We see an open gate.

A time of watching
is Now. Be alert
sharpen your eyes
and see what is coming.

Seer anointing,
prophetic voice
prayer authority
come forth and proclaim.

Apostles stand,
prophets speak
warriors intercede
the Body of Christ advances.

Moving in boldness
listening
watching
seeing the Hand of God.

His mantle is falling
miracles are occurring
with power and authority.
The time of waiting is Ending. . .

Our God is visible
as He surveys His army
ascended before Him
ready to descend to the battle.
Our God Reigns.
Judgment is coming.

Justice will prevail
o're all the earth...

Receive the seer anointed!

(Keat Wade 01/14/03)

Provision

Our wealth is in You…

In You, we are secure
let Your promises
be fulfilled
as our spirits soar.

Spirits first ascending
to the Throne Room
where we are washed over
with waves of intimacy.

Spirit filled
we can now receive
the wealth of Your provision
promised in Your Word.

All else will come
as we carry You with us
descending from the Throne room
equipped with Your anointed presence.

We claim Your promises
and reclaim the stolen property
of our inheritance
that was secreted from us.

Victory and the spoils belong to us…
(Keat Wade 01/21/03)

Wonder of Wonders

No knowledge of Him,
No invited presence,
As a child alone
But for God's grace
Claimed for her grandson
By grandmother Lucinda.

The keeping prevenient grace
With its restraining power
Kept this child of His
From destruction at the hands
Of the enemy
Strangely handcuffed.

Two other women
Triggered the transition
From prevenient to saving grace.
The romance of Rita
And praying mother, Ethel
Brought repentance and salvation on spiritual knees.

Years later suffering from loss
Of those ladies of divine influence
Came a new name, Judy
Now to be used to open
New realms of Glory in His presence
And release of the *SpiritedPen*.

Entering now, a new realm
Of basking in His presence

And steeped in intercession
We move forward and upward
Steadily rising, ascending
Preparing to descend to new battles.

New three-cord bonding
Walking alone into expanded territory
Always on the edge of unknown
Yet, without fear

Easily stepping to a new beat
Accompanied by heavenly drum rolls.

Lead On, Oh King Eternal!
(Keat Wade 01/25/03)

Wonder of Wonders – My paternal grandmother, from native American ancestry, stood firmly in her Christian faith. Even though she died on my second birthday and I cannot remember her, I feel she strongly contributed to my coming to a faith in Jesus because of her prevenient prayers for her grandson. Thank you Lucinda.

Do You Hear It A'Rumblin'? – After hearing Native American Dr. Suquinna, (Inuit) from Alaska, speak and after reading his writings, I was inspired to write this in response.

Do You Hear It A Rumblin'?

There is a new sound a comin'.
Comin' as never before
from the very Throne Room.
There is a shakin' and a rumblin'.

Thundering from heaven
His mighty army
marching, treading
prepared to crush the heads of His enemies.

The heavens are opening
through fasting and prayer
for those with eyes to see
and ears to hear.

The Lord of the Throne Room
is opening heavens doors
to pour out His fury.
Do you hear it a rumblin'?

His army awaits the word
from their Commander-in-Chief
to move into a new realm
of conquest for reclamation.

Prepare your heart for war.
Discard the weights that hold you
for God's army travels light,
unencumbered by earthly weapons.

Do you hear it a rumblin'?
Prepare to march
armed by the Spirit
with weapons indestructible.

The heavens are a rumbling'
                    (Keat Wade 01/26/03)

Harp and Bowl —
Heaven and Earth Connectors

The music symbolized in the harp
flows forth in undulating waves
inviting and calling
for the prayers of the anointed.
The prayerful voices rhythmically
rise beyond ceilings, beyond buildings
piercing middle heaven
to reach the Throne Room
filling the Golden Bowls
with the pure incense
from hearts of intercession
only to be poured back upon
a hurting world
soothing the hearts and cries
of the afflicted.
The new cries are absorbed
and infused into the music of the harpist
inspiring new intercessory cries
rising to refill golden bowls
already prepared for a new outpouring

Hear the harp!
Fill the bowls!

(Keat Wade 01/26/03)

His Name

From the beginning, all things being put in place a great God came down and formed from the elements of His creation man became a living soul at the hands of **Elohim**, the Creator.

We stand in awe in the knowledge of His creative power and humbled in the knowledge that we can know Him as He knows us for He is **Jehovah Hossenu**, our Maker.

How amazing, how wonderful is He who brought all life into being Who shepherds His creation and provides shelter and eternity in Him, **El Shaddai**, The Almighty God.

From our complacency and place of psuedo-rest we received a call to arms, to man our battle stations to follow **Jehovah Nissi**, the Lord, our Banner.

As the enemy seeks to strike fear in our hearts, we look to **Jehovah Shaloam**, our God of Peace assured the battle has long been decided.

Feeling lonely and forsaken, we are reminded by His Word that we can know **Jehovah Roah**, our Shepherd Who takes care of those who belong to Him.
Desperate, without resources or provision of our own we have one who provides, **Jehovah Yireh**, our provider Who possesses all the resources of heaven.

It is not within us to live perfection but He provides purity in our spirit and our devotion to Him in Holy living for He is **Jehovah Mekkadishkem**, The Lord Who Sanctifies You.

Nothing can overcome Him. No power is greater than His. He is forever and we are secure in Him even on the earth for He is, **The Most High God, El Elyon.**

There is no other that can compare. No name is adequate. Moses was humbled in His presence and dared to ask His name. The answer was sufficient then as now, **I AM that I AM.**

Fallen ill or deeply wounded hearts sinking into a chasm of doubt and confusion, we can rise above it with clean scars of supernatural release as we call upon **Jehovah Rapha**, The Lord that healeth thee.

As Gideon learned from God's own angel, The Lord is with thee, and simply replied, O my Lord, **Adonai-Jehovah**. He is the Lord over all of us, O My Lord.

With strife all around, it doesn't have to enter us as we walk not with the one who creates strife, but with the author of peace **Jehovah Sahalom**, The Lord is Peace.

From the beginning to the end from now and forever we rest in **El Odam**, The Everlasting God.

The One who is our redeemer, the Holy One of Israel Who has a host of angels as His army is truly **Jehovah Sabaoth**, The Lord of Hosts.

There is nothing hidden from You Who gave us eyes to see as we wait upon You, for **You-Are-the-God-Who-Sees**.

We do not fear where we are commanded to go in Your name for wherever we are, wherever we go, however dark or light we are assured by **Jehovah Shammah**, The Lord is There.

He gives us purity in heart, humility in spirit, the capacity to live a Holy life for He is **Jehovah Elohccnu, HOLY.**

Therefore, the days are coming says the Lord (Jer. 23:7) that they shall dwell in their own land for **Jehovah Tsidkenu**, The Lord Our Righteousness has spoken.

(Keat Wade 01/26/03)

He Gave Me a Golden Scepter

Awkwardly held
in my unpracticed hand
inspired by the holder alone
the lines were unclear
with empty words and broken phrases,
until heart and mind
were relinquished
to the giver of the gift.

The instrument of frustration
began to become steady,
now comfortably nestled
within the contours of my hand
and He named it
My SpirtedPen.

Devoted and dedicated to Him
the words began to flow
into phrases of wholeness
as we wrote together, God and I
allowing His words, now, to flow.
He proclaimed a new tool
in my hand, my Golden Scepter.
Fired in the trials of life
and refined through His grace.

(Keat Wade 01/27/03)

The Spirit of Interfaith

Hearts united in a common band
hands held high, praying, praising
to the One who inspires
the ladies of Interfaith.

Joining together, upholding one another
praising and interceding, standing in the Gap
God directs the hearts and minds
of the ladies of Interfaith.

Seed planted in the heart of Sister Martha
was tenderly nurtured and nourished,
slowly developing, coming to full term,
birthed and christened, Interfaith.

Twenty years of stretching, growing, feeding,
encouraging, reaching, ministering

ever sensitive to the One whom they serve,
with one goal, to please Him. . .

Is the spirit of Interfaith Prayer Fellowship.
(Keat Wade 02/03/03)

The Spirit of Interfaith - From the time we first came to San Diego 1996/1999-2009, we became a part of Interfaith Prayer Fellowship, founded and led by Sister Martha Featherstone. We learned much from the group of mostly African American women who love God and come together once a month to worship and serve our God. A wonderful enriching experience with those who have become treasured friends.

Lighthouses and Foghorns – As a youth I loved to read adventure stories involving the high seas. In traveling the work of the lighthouses and the sound of the foghorns in coastal areas became a fascination. In an unusual way they seemed like friends that if I watched and listened they would keep me safe.

Lighthouses and Foghorns

The beam sweeps across the skies
again and again in timed rotation
comfortingly familiar to all
protecting those who ply the seas.

As fog creeps over the watery byways
mariners slow and peer closely
through the darkness to catch sight
of the lifesaving sweeping light.

As the fog gathers too thick to pierce the darkness
silence reigns as lookouts lean against their
restraints
to catch the sound from the unseen but constant
sentinel of the sea rolling out the moan of its
unique, mournful foghorn voice.

Brightly beaming or eerily sounding
through the darkness, each signal goes out
to wary mariners, warning them away

from treacherous reefs, guiding them to safe
harbors.
(Keat Wade 02/04/03)

It's Time Has Come

A poem of dedication for the book
Take the Name of Jesus With You
by
Judy Garlow Wade

The seed was planted those many years ago
and a long gestation period began.
Tho' oft delayed in development
it's life was never doubted
nor it's coming questioned.
Slowly growing within, by thought
and divine visitation
the files of the mind slowly
filled waiting to be opened
to final action when all was in order.

Everything and everyone coming together
in time, place and order
the seed began to germinate, rapidly
having been properly nourished
and the earth prepared across three states.

In His time and order
in this southwestern gateway
vision sharpened and cleared
as the files overflowed onto the printed page.
The final stage had begun.

Following years of preparation
crossing many paths of those whom He had
prepared
to speak into a chosen, readied, hungry heart
each stamping the pages of their preparation
that were gladly received and recorded.

The baby has been birthed
and will now take on a life of its own
as the loving Father parents it
into the sharp instrument that He intended
to break up untended, neglected soil.

May new seeds
now fall on fallow ground
prepared through an obedient birthmother
with her faithful midwives at her side
under the shadow of Elohim....

And they shall *Take the Name of Jesus With Them*.
(Keat Wade 04/01/03)

Where Your Spirit Flows – After seeing a video of the worship of the Christian indigenous people of New Zealand, I could feel the power of the Maori warriors in their dance and these words came forth.

Where the Spirit Flows

My hearts leaps as I hear the sounds
When worship bursts forth
Releasing Your Fire
Where the Spirit flows.

The beat resounds echoing
The rhythm of Your heart
As the dancers swirl
Where Your Spirit flows.

Your prophet singers
Reflect Your hearts desire
As we ascend in our worship
Into Your rivers where the Spirit flows.

Higher and higher we swirl
Lifted on the wings of worship
Into a new heavenly realm
Where Your Spirit floods and fills....

Engulfed, immersed in the placid,
Yet, moving, swirling lake of Your desire
Filling us, equipping us
Flowing in Your Spirit for descent.

Strengthened, ready for the battles
That we shall surely win
Because we have been
Where Your Spirit fully flows.

The battles rage in this earthly realm
Against our endless resources in You
As we descend for battle, yet to ascend again
To the place where Your Spirit flows.

Swirling upward on the wings of worship
You reveal to us our endless,
Unbroken line of supply
When we ascend to the realm ...
Where Your Spirit flows.

(Keat Wade 04/12/03)

The Wilderness of His Love

Be not dismayed
when I call you into the wilderness
for it is into My home
the wilderness of my love.

There is a rest in my wilderness
that man alone cannot know
for you shall have a foretaste
of your heavenly home, prepared for you.

Remember the road I promised?
My wilderness is not an abandoned place
as you thought, but the center of who I AM
and where I dwell....
And My River shall run through it.

(Keat Wade 07/11/03)

The Wilderness of His Love - During the fellowship celebration of Shabbat at Billie and Darrell Alexander's this poem was conceived, grew to full term, and was birthed in the span of two hours. How wonderful are His revelations and timing.

The House Within

Though not so by design
The windows were now gray
Clouded by subtle, creeping layer upon layer
Keeping out redeeming light.

The dust of despair
Covered everything within
Creating the darkness
Of foreboding corners.

Powers unseen and unnoticed
By its keeper, the house
Reeked of silent, clinging deception
Unnoticed by the occupant, presumed alone.

The uninvited presence
Crept as a vapor through
Portals left carelessly open by he
For whom the dwelling was created.

Near despair of hopelessness I met the Presence
Of True Light that dispels the shadows,
Illuminating the dark corners
Revealing the interloper of my soul.

The true light of this new Presence
Would come in and dwell with me on my bidding
If only I acknowledge and love Him
As the Lord of the house.

Covenant in place, cleaning began
Setting the invading guest to flight,
Corners brightened as windows cleared
And He, the light, filled that place.

As the presence of the enemy of my soul
Had darkened my house
So the new Lord of my life
Lightened the house, for He is Light.

All entry portals secure
Windows clear
Now lighted from within
My house is restored…

And I bow in His continual presence
…in The House Within.
(Keat Wade 07/13/03)

On Wings As Eagles

If we were an eagle safely perched
on the bluffs high above valley floors,
conflicts, tensions, the misunderstood
seen from such lofty heights
would give clearer visions
for humble reconciliation.

An even fuller picture
can be seen as we launch out
dropping below the craggy perch
allowing us to catch the upward flow
to circle and soar, climbing on invisible steps
ever rising, moving current to upward current.

Circling, soaring, catching new drafts
of clean, powerful resurgence
lifting, entering lonely places
rarely experienced, reaching
heavenly heights, catching a glimpse
of what He sees on our tainted land.

Worship carries us
on wings, as those of the eagles
to those rarified realms of the Spirit
spending time in intimacy with Him
now, seeing clearly
through the eyes of the Savior.

(Keat Wade 08/06/03)

2004

It Is Coming!

It is coming,
that anointing you desire.

It is coming
as your spirit joins Mine
that I may coach and infuse you
for release of that
which I have placed within you.
It is that which you need, no other.

Lean close to Me, listen carefully.
For I am preparing you, as no other.
Yield your mind, your thoughts,
your knowledge, your heart
to the mold that I have prepared for only you.

As our spirits blend
through your yieldedness
and My love for you,
Your words will flow forth
as a tolling bell, ringing clear
resonating the beat of My heart
as those who have ears to hear are drawn
into the waters where My Spirit flows.

You are my chosen instrument, equipped,
guiding the builders of My threshing machine

which will contribute to a great harvest in due time
as My heavenly barns are filled with those snatched
from the fire and ushered into My kingdom
into the season of forever.

And I will say,
"Well done!"
(Keat Wade 01/27/04)

Hope Deferred

A lonely circling path created endless spirals

Going nowhere, dangling the goal
Of unfulfilled dreams called hope deferred
Just beyond the outstretched hand.

Allowing a glimmer of wistful anticipation,
By the shadowy presence, tantalizingly providing
Just enough to keep one trying, stretching for the prize,
Always, just out of reach of the trembling hand.

As a spark from within, though slowly fading,
Continued to glow, a heavier, darker image
Appeared overshadowing the scene
Strangely bringing light pulsating from its form, a cross...
Transcending hope deferred
To hope restored
Bringing hope fulfilled
In the hand now grasping, in triumph,
My very soul!
(Keat Wade 02/03/04)

Read the Wind

Perched high on rugged bluffs

overlooking valley floors
seeing through keen eyes
designed for discernment
of signs and wonders below
he reads the winds, unseen.

Facing the rhythmic, flowing currents he senses
the increasing rush of forceful winds.
Waiting for just the right moment
he extends his wings, leans forward
allowing himself to be launched and carried
in faith by winds, unseen.

Lord, give us the capacity to read the winds
and the discernment, in faith, to extend our wings
and allow the flow of Your breathing, Living Words
to give them lift to soar, riding, without effort,
on the winds of Your love
into our eternal destiny.
(Keat Wade 03/07/04)

I Am the Land

I was created for you
But was not respected
For what I am
And why I was formed. . .
I am the land.

Intended as a gift, yet contended for
By spirits of greed and power;
I was scorched, overridden,
Stained by innocent blood. . .
Yet, I remain, the land.

With no recognition of the giver above
And the authority of the keeper,
I was relinquished to the challenger below
As my possessor, yet . . . I remain the land.

Fight for me!
Reclaim me!
Be reconciled to me,
Redeem me, cleanse me
. . . For I am your land.

When will you rise up
And honor the Giver
And challenge the unlawful possessor?
I am your inheritance. Reclaim me,
That He who made me may come and dwell
With us. . . I am the Land.

(Keat Wade 03/14/04)

And the Waters Shall Flow

Open the floodgates of heaven, O Lord
That your rivers may flow over Your mountain
And waterfalls may splash forth
As deep calls deep at the sound,
Calling the deceived and dying
To come under the flow of Your saving grace and
healing hands-
May they know your loving kindness by day
And hear Your night song
Joining the prayerful wooing
Of the God of our lives.

May Your mountain stand forever
As a sentinel, a beacon to all
Calling them to Your refreshing streams
Eternally flowing from this mountain,
To those who walk in obedience with You,
Through the washed valleys of Your Presence
Living Testimonies to Your deliverance
From the enemy's clouds of deception,
Winds of destruction and martyr's pyres
Safe In the streams from heavenly waterfalls.
(Keat Wade 03/21/04)

And the Waters Shall Flow - Psalm 42:7-8
Deep calls unto deep at the noise
of Your waterfalls;
All Your waves and billows have gone over me.

8) The Lord will command His loving kindness in
the daytime,
And in the night His sons shall be with me -
A prayer to the God of my life.

Can You Hear Our Mountain Sing? -
"Sing O heavens!
Be joyful, O earth!
And break out in singing, O mountains!
For the Lord has comforted His people,
And will have mercy on His afflicted." Isaiah
49:13

Can You Hear the Mountains Sing?

Walking and praying the ridges,
speaking scripture along downward paths,
around the structure of His abiding;
can you hear the mountain sing?

Coming with clean hands and pure hearts
require much looking within
that any unrighteousness be revealed
to clear canals for listening for heavenly vibrations.

As truth, righteousness and order are reestablished
in the hearts of the keepers of the mountain
the vibrations will grow and swell to a crescendo
and the mountain will break into singing.

Let it begin with me, Lord
and among the hearts of your people
that Your name may be glorified
at the sound of our mountain singing.

Look within, Act in obedience, Listen…
It is about to begin.
(Keat Wade 03/27/04)

Out of the Cave – This poem was partially inspired
by the reading of Isaiah's experience in running from
the wrath of Jezebel in panic after his great victory
over the priests of Baal. Exhausted, he took refuge
in a cave. From there my imagination and the Lord's
teaching took over. This reminded me how He had
lead me out of my cave into His light.

Out of the Cave

From deep within my cave
The light appears a very small light
In my darkness, seemingly safe
From what I cannot see beyond its circle.

As I move toward the light
More is exposed of what is there
Yet, I shrink away in fear
Of what I cannot see.

The blackness is consuming
And yet, the light draws me forward
With a strange sense of peace
Despite the clutching hands of darkness.

Drawing closer, the circle grows wider
The fear of the unknown
Grows strangely paled, exposed
To the growing light.

Now all I have to fear

Is in the sinister darkness,
Once my refuge
Now being exposed by the light.

No ordinary light is this
For it bursts forth
Being released from within me
As the source is made known.
How blind we are to light
As the bat and the mole.
We are no longer deceived
By darkness, but revel in His light.
(Keat Wade 03/27/04)

Wings of the Dawn
Reflections on Psalm 139

Oh it is good, Lord
to rise on the wings of the dawn
And soar with You.

As we lift our hearts
Our spirit ascends to the edge of heaven
Where we are bathed in Your presence.

When our spirit falters
We descend to the depths
Yet, You are there.

There is nowhere we can go
Foreign to Your Spirit as we
See through anointed eyes, on the wings of the
dawn.

You know each movement,
Our thoughts before we speak,
Your Spirit abides from dawn to dawn as we ride
their wings

Light and dark are the same to You,
You light the way by Your presence
As we rise and soar on the wings of each dawn.

You knew us before we were.
By Your design we are wonderfully made
To rise, soar, ascend rejoicing in You.

Search us oh, Lord,
Test us, cleanse us.
Lead us in Your way that on the wings of each dawn
We may ascend eternally with you
to abide above all yesterday's dawns.
(Keat Wade 04/01/04)

In This Place

Softly glowing light
emanating from a peaceful presence
creates an encompassing comfort
zone in this place.

The journey has been long and arduous,
yet, my arrival was instant,
seemingly never gone
from this place.
There is a rhythm
matching my heart's beat,
soothing my very soul
on entering this place.

Reaching for a desired unknown,
drawn by that invisible presence
by irresistible waves of warmth and love
we experience that which we find in no other place.

Overwhelmed, we begin to see,
first, only clouded images,
but then, as if face to face, clearly,
experiencing Him who calls us from . . .
this place, the chambers of His heart.

(Keat Wade 10/10/04)

In the Golden Glow of His Glory

Spirits throbbing with expectancy
shine through the uplifted faces
ready to be bathed in the golden flow
from the bowl glowing with His Glory.

Come, let us move with haste
into new realms beyond the edge of our imagination
approaching the holy of holies
arm in arm with He who is calling.

Personal and intimate with His corporate Body
He gives experience we cannot describe
walking where we have not been
where nothing remains the same
. . . Only Him!
(Keat Wade 10/24/04)

Symphony from His Heart

Let the symphony begin
when the prelude softly lifts
as we enter
the sacred chamber, reserved.
Worship rises in harmony
with the increasing throbbing
of our Father's Heart
as it draws ours into rhythm with His.
Rising in crescendos of love
from chamber to chamber
echoing through the halls
of Heaven and Earth. . .
is a symphony from His heart.
(Keat Wade 11/03/04)

The Breaking of the Dawn – As we were coordinating a prayer room at a Mission America Conference, Judy shared a vision and the visual picture appeared in my mind as described here.

The Breaking of the Dawn

The disappearing silence of darkness
that overshadowed the land from sea to sea
was rent by a sweeping stroke of the
sword in His hand,
opening the way for light to spread, east to west.
The sweep of the sword continued
with a coastal circle
that completed the separation
of the darkness from the land.

A new "breaking of the dawn"
swept across the land,
as the wagons of old, ushering in the new,
bringing the brightness of His light . . .
In the time of His eternal NOW!
(Keat Wade 11/21/04)

2005

Eternal Glimpses

As my voice rose
in endless echoes of worship and adoration,
the curtain parted
allowing entry for the one
who held my hand in a gentle, yet, strong grasp
as we stepped onto an untrodden path
lined by a spectrum of flowers
seemingly created just for my garden
as it wound a circuitous route
in pursuit of a sweet smelling aroma,
(possessing a near life form),
hugging the banks of gently flowing waters
that, as one peers down into it,
reflects the glory of heaven above,
emanating from the One who dwells there.

Only a briefly delicious, yet, eternal moment,
was a glimpse into that heavenly realm granted
to become a timeless snapshot experience
permanently embossed
upon the memory of this weary traveler . . .
desiring more
(Keat Wade 01/13/05)

My Praise, They Shall Declare
[They shall declare My praise. Isaiah 43:21]

My breath excites the wind, the wind of change.
Almost imperceptible at first,
then a stirring felt lightly upon the face.
Flags hanging upon their posts
Begin to stir, unfurling
opening, flowing, then cracking
to the rhythm of the wind
Ushering a change
only sensed by the perceivers
whose voices rise in a new sound, yet unheard,
but now resounding in echoes
carried by His breath, responding
to His declaration, "They shall declare My Praise."
                    (Keat Wade 02/08/05)

Wilderness Unto Wilderness

Behold, I will do a new thing,
Now it shall spring forth,
Shall ye not know it?
I will even make a road in the wilderness
Arid rivers in the desert

The beast of the field will honor Me,
The jackals and the ostriches,
Because I give waters in the wilderness
And rivers in the desert,
To give drink to My people, My chosen.
This people I have formed for Myself
They shall declare My praise.
Isaiah 43:19-21 (NKJV)

Old tasks completed, new exodus begins
from the generation of Moses to the
now of our lives.
However great the struggle, the Lord is with us
providing His manna and living water
lifting our spirits and nourishing our bodies
as we move toward our destiny,
We move through each wilderness
honoring Him while resting in His peace.
Each new challenge that He brings us through
builds confidence and boldness
As we move in Him
From wilderness unto wilderness.

We struggle and cry, "Why"
While He chips away the impurities
That would hinder us in the next testings
As He shows us the blessing of His provision
In our wilderness experience where
we grow stronger,
More determined, as we move
... through wilderness unto wilderness.

(Keat Wade 02/08/05)

If This Land Could Speak

If this land could speak
What would it say of its history,
its inhabitants from the beginning?
Tales of woe and of joy
would surely be a part of the story
as the unfolding spills out
helping us to know its cry.

What groups peopled the land;
And what game
roamed this expanse,
Providing food, tools and comfort
Through endless seasons
and their winds of change
That swept from horizon to horizon?

What blood stained this soil?
Yours, oh, ancient original dwellers;
coupled with those who came to see
and perhaps, possess the land,
bringing dispute, distrust
leading to conflict and killing
that has not ended.

Meant to sustain its people,
the land has suffered corruption
at the hands of all
who have trod upon it
And now cries out
For redemption through

Repentance allowing
the flow of original blessings
As peace settles
upon the land
Through reconciliation
both, with each other
And their Creator, God.

Then, the Lord may speak
peace and harmony upon
both the land and its inhabitants.

(Keat Wade 02/17/05)

If This Land Could Speak began to form in my mind as we drove across New Mexico and Arizona.

The Wonder of Bonnie Brae – In preparation for the 100th Anniversary of the Azusa Street Revival of 1906, we visited the Bonnie Brae House where the revival began. We spent much of one day there worshipping with a team. This inspiration came as a result of the spirit of worship that we felt and as we reviewed the history of that place.

The Wonder of Bonnie Brae

On the porch of a humble house numbered 216,
In a special place in a special time
Stood a black man with only one good eye
That was aflame with the power that was
coming from within.
Sparked by a new found Spirit called Holy,
Spoke boldly of God's
Plan for those with ears to hear
And eyes to see.
Growing in the fullness of this move
Of the anointing upon him
A spark that set aflame, the hearts of people
Birthed a movement that cannot be stopped
Though it has survived opposition
Like unto that of Bible times
In ancient lands, where
Twelve men also obeyed
And set in motion a course of events
That nineteen hundred six years later
Gave voice to a man named Seymour
Whose words, known and unknown,

Still echo down Bonnie Brae Street
Touching and filling hearts
Of those who dare enter
A house now simply called. . .
Bonnie Brae.
(Keat Wade 03/10/05)

Sound, Sand and Time

The sound of surf beneath darting gulls
along once anticipated sandy beaches,
have, by passing months and years,
proved to be miles of shifting roadways;
now memories represented symbolically
in our lives as...SANDS OF TIME,
always remaining the NOW of His time
while the vanishing line of sea and sand
continue to disappear together
ever subtly reshaping our land.

Still side by side, sand and time stretch on
with you like the sea,
and me like the land.
With a new sound ringing in our ears
. . . life continues to reshape as we move along,
still surpassing any good thing I know.

(Keat Wade, 03/21/05)

It Happens At the Cross

At the feet of Jesus
at the foot of the cross
I died; to myself, my life,
and all became His
. . . at the foot of the cross.

At the feet of Jesus
remembering His cross
I am taught by Him
about life and truth
. . . at the foot of the cross.

I shall ever be transfixed
by the image of His torn and tortured body
upon those rugged timbers
sacrificed in innocence, for my guilt
. . . forgiven at the foot of the cross.

The cross stands empty,
as, indeed, is His borrowed tomb
that I may know of His great love
each time I return
. . . to the foot of the cross.

May each reader of these words,
in turn, meet Him,
learn of Him,
accept Him, through the reality found
. . . at the foot of the cross.
(Keat Wade 03/27/05)

And It Shall Cover the Earth - Written for and read at the Global Day of Prayer, 2005 held at Oceanside, California Amphitheater at the ocean's edge.

And It Shall Cover the Earth

A small spark in African tinder
Fanned by the wind of His Spirit,
A holy fire spread across a city, a nation,
Now igniting a continent.

The fanned sparks leap across borders
To new cities, nations
And confinements as a perpetual advancement
That will not be quenched,
But continually fanned
Consuming the globe.

One dream, shared, became a passion
Destined to cover the earth
With the sound of the Lord
Rising as one voice from our global day of prayer
. . . Let the nations rejoice!
(Keat Wade 05/01/05)

Little Girl Within

Nine years young
as her life hung in the balance
while she was lifted
to heavenly realms
and met the one
who gave her a mission
bound to dominate her life.

Returned to her body,
never to be the same,
as memory remained fixed
on one who comforted her
with a promise of intimate
lifetime relationship
that would be filled with
supernatural impartation.

Though now in an adult body
the little girl within
who sat on Jesus lap,
receiving revelation,
and was given ageless, divine insight
and wisdom for a lifetime
now enabled to minister and impart.

The little girl,
Preserved by a moment in time,
lives on in an adult heart and body.
Increasing in wisdom and the delight
of his continual presence.

The little girl will never grow old nor weary
because of an indisputable heavenly encounter.
(Keat Wade 05/03/05)

Little Girl Within - Written by inspiration from the life of our friend, Pat Bahr. At age 9 she was struck by a car while riding her bicycle. While in the Queen of Angels Hospital (now the Dream Center) in Los Angels she had a near-death experience and went to heaven. She describes vividly what she learned from Jesus.

Over whelmed

Who will control,
Task or Master?

All in the Master's plan
Excitement fills my being
As it is revealed, then comes
the reality of overwhelmed.

Weighty, weighty is the task
Burdening my mind, heart, and soul.
The task is too great, I need help
lest I be swept away, overwhelmed.

Only a determination within my spirit
Prompted by sources untapped,
Led me into the now of this time
one step at a time.

Step by step the walls before me
become less formidable,
less threatening,
not so overwhelming.

The path behind me grows longer
Than the remaining path before me
Giving occasional glimpses of
Remaining tasks, less overwhelming.

Within reach, now, is the goal.
Bolstered by unseen, unknown strength,

He now reveals how the task was completed.
Because I have been overwhelmed by Him.
(Keat Wade 05/12/05)

The Power of Silence

For the natural man the absence of sound cried for
discernable vibrations
that stimulate his senses
and allays his fear of...silence.

He has yet to learn
of the power of silence
in the spiritual man
as he waits before his God.

Only in the silence
do we hear
His "still small voice"
drawing us, speaking, teaching.

How we need to honor Him
in our worship as we
prepare to rest and listen
in the silence of His Presence.

It is there that we commune
Spirit to spirit
while He eternally washes over us
with His Divinity.

Washed over by the Spirit of the Divine, refreshed,
empowered, emboldened,
we move forth following His command
in granted authority over that entrusted to us.
(Keat Wade 06/12/05)

The Silence

Be still and listen to the stillness,
As we praise Him
With our heart and spirit,
Building to a crescendo. . .of SILENCE.

In reverential quietude
With singular focus
Something builds within some
While the awe of His presence envelopes all.

No words or thoughts
As He fills our being
With the essence of His presence,
Now, forever etched upon our hearts.

"Be still and know that *I AM* God."
(Keat Wade 07/02/05)

The New Sound

From a whisper to a crescendo,
sounds vary, rise and fall
in pitch, tone, and intensity
as words form or music flows.

New vibrations in unique patterns
are swelling, swirling, flowing
within us as an infant cry
pushing to be birthed and burst forth.

Through our praise and worship
drawing Him into intimacy
around and within us, building
a new vibration, a precursor, ready to break forth.

Be released Oh sound,
as we open our mouths
to be filled by Him in new expression
to burst forth. And we will know
. . .the Sound of the Lord.

(Keat Wade 07/27/05)

He Is Our Peace – These scriptures inspired the following poem.

"Peace I leave with you, My peace I give to you;
not as the world gives do I give to you.
Let not your heart be troubled,
neither let it be afraid." John 14:27

I will both lie down in peace, and sleep;
For You alone, O Lord, make me dwell in safety. Ps
4:8

For He Himself is our peace. . . (Eph 2:14a

He Is Our Peace

Not of ourselves
but only in Him
and He in us
do we live, love, and be in peace.

Such peace surely does
surpass all understanding
as we live and work in this world
with a hint of what is to come.

Abide forever in me
that I may know
the intimacy of the Father
and know Your perfect peace.

Break forth O Spirit
within me, that
brings forth
Your everlasting peace.
(Keat Wade 08/10/05)

Be Still – For over a year our prayer meetings had been focused on waiting on the Lord, by design, in silence. This poem reflects a perception of how the Lord might look upon our worshipfully waiting in His presence. It suggests joyous response from the heavenly beings surrounding the throne.

Be Still

As the music of worship fades,
Your silence of praise
Rises in pleasant waves
Arriving as a crescendo,
Caressing the windows of heaven,
And I am pleased.

I love the depth of your devotion
In the intimacy of quiet
That we share while I speak
Into your spirit and whisper,
"Tarry a little longer.
Listen, hear the sound of heaven."

You have been so near experiencing
The fullness of My sound and the whirling eddies
Rippling out from heavenly beings surrounding you,
Waiting to be released in the stillness
Of the crescendo of your silence.
Now, as never before, experience Me.
Be still and know that I AM God.

(Keat Wade 08/15/05)

Quakes, Shakes, and Other Phenomenon – After our stealth journey to an area of high seismic activity (earthquakes), where we carried out an assignment received in a dream which included specific coordinates, the quaking stopped. The quakes occurred as a swarm which is a sequence of earthquakes that happen in a relatively short period of time in the same general area. This poem was written out of that experience.

Quakes, Shakes, and Other Phenomenon

Coming in jolts, tremors and swarms
The earth shakes and trembles.

Set aside time for Me and listen
I'm trying to get your attention.

With cleansed hearts
Pray and prepare for My signs and wonders.

Turn would-be tragedy
Into the miraculous as I respond to you.

Be still and know
That I AM still the one in control.

My voice will come in many ways,
Listen, Listen, Listen, Listen!
(Keat Wade 09/09/05)

Across the Fire – As I read the account in scripture of Peter's denial of Jesus, I began to think what it must have been like when their eyes met? I saw the picture of their eyes meeting across the fire. I felt as if I were the one at whom He looked. I will always remember the disappointment and hurt in His eyes.

Across the Fire

Our eyes met across the fire
before the coming dawn
was announced by
the prophetic sound of the cock's crow.

My heart was pierced, my spirit, broken,
as my memory was flooded
with the weight of His words,
. . . deny three times before the cock crows.

Yet, no accusation
in those penetrating eyes
that pierced my heart and soul;
only love and offered forgiveness.

How could that be?
It could only come through
the one by whom we are humbled
at the foot of an executioner's cross.

No love was ever expressed more
than through the one whose eyes

met mine in the midst the an accusing crowd
beside the fire which does not warm.

But God, . . .

The power of His gaze offers healing
to broken spirits, wounded hearts, and lost souls
when eyes meet . . . *across the fire*.
(Keat Wade 09/20/05)

Awash with His Sound

Months, years in the coming
Was the sound that filled that place.

We had waited so long,
Some, more than others.

As His selected ones came together
The night was different.

The light trail of a rocket
Led one to the gathering.
While another was awakened
From a sound sleep
And could not return
To that place of rest
Until his wife's return
From God's gathering place.

Another had experienced
What he considered to be
The worst week of his life.
Yet, he left filled, satisfied, running over.

The atmosphere was fragrant
With His presence
From beginning to end
As the sounds began to swirl,
Intertwining in the form of persons
Being released into Him.
When it seemed that

The atmosphere could
Contain no more
His angel moved
To the keyboard
Lighted from within and without.

The sound of the ancient
Blended with the spirit of vibrancy of the new
Rose and fell
Swirling and caressing
Over and among us
Calling forth a corporate sound
That none had heard before.
In that moment peace and unity
Ruled over the city
As all moved to new levels
Where none had walked ... but God!
(Keat Wade 09/23/05)

Behold the Days

One hand clutching
My garment's hem
While each hold to the other
Weaving a strong cord.

In My plan this is right
For the day is coming
When you have no other.
I AM sufficient.

You will minister
But never out of My reach
Or beyond My voice for I have said,
"I will never leave nor forsake you."

You are mine, bought with a price
For My purposes
For such a time as this
As My countdown grows short.

Behold the days
And hold to me
As My plan unfolds
Into eternity.

(Keat Wade, 10/21/05)

Mute Before the Throne

Something has changed.
Whirling dancers wind to a stop;
Voices of worshipful joy fade into silence;
We fall mute before the Throne.

A new level of worship
Fills the atmosphere
Like fog moving ashore
Filling each heart.

Only desiring to continue,
We enter new realms of Glory
With no path back,
Nor one desired.

The Glory of brief encounters
Now become our complete existence
While our whole being remains
Mute before the Throne.

Life as has been known no longer exists.
He shows us how to live without walls
Filled and surrounded by Him
Living in His Spirit... MUTE Before the THRONE!

Our Sound Must Resound
Throughout the Universe,
- Sent from the Throne -
- Mute No Longer -

Planted there, cultured there, perfecting there,
The sound cultured within us,
Pearling forth, ever expanding
As it goes forth opening wide,
Reflecting translucent sound
Penetrating the senses, wirelessly transcendent.
(Keat Wade 11/16/05)

Within the Depths

Echoing through the chambers comes the invitation
To rise from the depths of yourself
To enter the depths of His love
Into the heart chamber intimately designed for you.

Come My beloved, My child,
For I long to share My heart in the pure love
I have for you, as these chambers
Echo our mutual loneliness for one another.

The abandoned child is forever drawn
Into My chambered sanctuary
Never again to experience abandoned loneliness
Totally enwrapped, consumed in My intimate love.

The heavens cry out and rejoice
As you each hear My cry
To enter your special chamber
Within the many rooms of My Heart.

My love songs whisper through the corridors
And softly enter each chamber
Carrying My intimate healing words,
"You are Mine and I am yours."

(Keat Wade 11/21/05)

2006

Becoming the NOW

Prophetic voices so long looking into
That which is to come,
Now speak of them
In the NOW time of God,
No longer forthcoming
But evolving into the today of history.
(Keat Wade 01/20/06)

He Cometh

We receive the Word of the coming Someone
Bringing blessing and assurance
Of Your gifts and Your presence.

Discernment and freedom from fear,
Grant, O, Lord,
That we may see clearly.

We bow in obedience
Seeking strength to withstand
Efforts to distract.

With our eyes upon you
We wait, senses alert,
For what is to come.

We stand on alert
To move into appointed ministry
Both seen and unseen. . .*Come!*
(Keat Wade 01/30/06)

Walk of Love

Let all evil be far from me
In thought, word, or deed,
As I remain steadfast in desire,
To walk as he walked, as He walked, in Love.

Let darkness be dispelled
Make manifest Your presence and expose evil
Through the fruit of the Spirit
As we walk in Light.

Not unwise, but full of understanding,
In steps of watchfulness and caution,
Filled with the Spirit,
Speaking, singing,
Giving thanks, submitting
As we walk in Wisdom.

Therefore,
Walk in love as I am Love,
In light as I am Light,
In wisdom through submitting.
. . . these three guiding us
As we walk and lead
In our pursuit of Him.
(Keat Wade 02/13/06, Based on Ephesians 5:1-21)

As the Sound of Many Waters –On the morning
of March 23, 2006 I was drawn to the words of
Revelation 1:14-15, especially 15b "…and His voice

as the sound of many waters." Visualizing the many forms of moving water the imagery began to form as I wrote the first stanzas.

March 25th, I heard in my spirit, ". . .the deep placid waters that show no stirring or waves, where I say My voice is strongest, puzzles you." The deep waters are fed and continually restored by springs of water from deep within the bed of the waters. From those springs of living water comes His Voice speaking strongest but not necessarily loudest.

March 27th During a worship service I heard, ". . .The glassy surface of the deep still waters exude silence and silence alone to the unprepared ear." Only the attuned spirit and trained ear will hear clearly.

As the Sound of Many Waters

It may be heard in the crashing thunder
of surf breaking through coastal rocky shore
to hammer hard upon the sand.
It speaks softly in the rising mists
above the waterfalls
or whispers amid the gurgling
of tumbling mountain stream
seeking serenity in deep placid waters.

In the quiet of the placid deep
It speaks the loudest
as we have ears to hear
and a willing spirit to receive.

.

It is there for the hearing
by those prepared to receive it
for His voice is
"…as the sound of many waters."
Will you miss it?
Prepare in worship, partake of Him.
In the essence of His presence
be lifted into the level of His dwelling.
(Keat Wade 03/25/06)

Go for the Gold

In the form of golden talc
It settled, invisibly upon

Those chosen worthy
As an anointing presence.

Twenty-four carat pure
Divinely prepared
For this hour
And for this purpose.

Phenomenon, mystery of God
Special manifestation
Declaring the relationship
With the Father above.

No striving will bring it
No crying will merit it
His dying provided it
If we will receive it

(Keat Wade 04/1/06)

Faithful Housewives – From her circle of friends, Georgette had taken a group of women, including my wife, to Los Angeles for the television taping of the Dr Phil Show. During the interview Dr. Phil took Georgette off guard by asking her the name of the group. Although this was a casual collection of friends, she spontaneously announced "Faithful Housewives" and it stuck.

Faithful Housewives

One woman's creative thought
bringing together women who
love their husbands and children,
birth announced in a studio
those lovingly called
. . . Faithful Housewives.

Spreading joy
in a spirit of love
for each other
and sharing it all
in prayer and love
of the One who unifies them.

Encouragers, lending support,
mentoring, while modeling
their message of
loving their husbands and children,
their Biblical mandate.

(Keat Wade 04/05/06)

Acknowledged by Him

Though ignored we persist
Knowing that our Father
Who sees, shows us favor
As we sing His words back to Him.

We rejoice with those who seek Him
And remember His work in us
And the promise
Of what is to come.

We sing to Him the new song
He has placed within our hearts
As we delight in anointed assignments
As we walk with Him.

As we tarry, He smiles
And points the way
One step at a time
Into greater realms of His glory.

Greater is the destiny
Of those who fear not
Stepping into the NEW
That He has in store.

(Keat Wade 04/12/06)

On the Wings of Your Wind

Whether in storm or in favor
From dark caverns or Heaven's treasuries
The winds blow destruction
Or soothing blessings,
For You ride on the wings of the wind.

Lord, bid me come
That I, too, may ride
On the wings of the wind
That rumbles from heaven to earth
As You ride the wind.
Fill my sails with Your breath
As You purge, cleanse and purify,
Even destroy those who defy You
And are drawn in to the vortex of Your fury
As You direct the winds that You ride.

Now let the winds out of Your treasuries
Stir and grow in a powerful force
For those who wait upon You
To see the golden glow of Your Glory
In the winds upon which You ride.

(Keat Wade 09/17/06)

2007

Like No Other

What I have bestowed
is like no other you have known,
a unique sound in the universe.
You are the sound,
I have made you
unlike any other.

It must not be diluted,
only strengthened,
as your sound swirls upward,
your voices soaring
reflecting pure hearts
seeking only Me.

As I am drawn to reach down
To the upward reach of your spirit
I connect with you
and we have fusion
of heart and Spirit.
Now, WE ARE . . .

Stylized by I AM . . .
Like no other!
(Keat Wade 08/12/07)

Walking Words – The concept of putting action to our words was my inspiration.

Walking Words

Filled with My words
walk the paths set before you.
with anointed feet, each step
resonating what is planted within you
as your steps echo the beat of My Heart
to those who follow and those you meet.

Let spoken words come forth
as I direct and your spirit hears,
in turn, reflecting the double beat of our hearts
filling our atmosphere with angelic sounds
joined by the voices of a multitude
of delirious heavenly hosts.

The sounds from earthly footsteps
join anointed healing sounds penetrating
the most reluctant hearts
and resistant souls
brought to moments of Truth
bowing to the sound of walking words.

(Keat Wade 08/14/07)

When Silence Thunders

Stop! Look! Listen!

Let the stillness reign.
Watch for My clues.
Listen that I may reveal
That which I choose.

In the quietude, focus on Me.
With eagle eyes scan your domain.
Look for My manifestation
Even in unexpected places.

Listen with all the capacity of your senses;
Ears, mind, spirit …
Even to the surface of your body,
Hear Me.

Do not be discouraged
By the silence
When nothing seems to be speaking
For I am at work.

Be not dismayed.
Time is only your limit.
I am there and will manifest
In My time.

Stop! Look! Listen!
(Keat Wade 11/08/07)

Vision from Michelangelo – During a prayer meeting the Lord gave me a vision of the reaching hands from the painting on the ceiling of the Sistine Chapel. I saw the reaching hands and the words of this poem flowed onto the page

Vision from Michelangelo

A hand reaching down, index finger extended
As if pointing and, yet, more like reaching for contact
With the hand reaching up, finger also extended.

The gap is not great, yet, a definite separation

Allowing an occasional spark to jump downward
In a brief surge of communion, spirit to spirit.

To He who is reaching down there is a desire
For greater contact even fusion with the extended fingers
If the one reaching up can only extend a little higher.

The wisdom gained through the occasional spark
Inspires the reaching one who begins to recognize
A mutual desire/need for a continuous flow, spirit to spirit.

An act of sacrifice on a cross of wood broke the barrier
For the reaching hands to fuse into a flowing conduit

Allowing the reaching one's heart to come into heart
rhythm . . .

Beat by beat by beat by beat . . .
In rhythm which flows from the Father's heart.
                                    (Keat Wade 12/08/07)

2008

Walk In His Light

And He spoke
Walk in My Light.

Turn from darkness.
Face My Light.

No more see negatives,
Only positives.

For there is no room for your shadows
In My Light.

Then only will your see yourself
As I see you.

My desire is that you walk into
The Light of My Glory.

That you will see as I see,
Hear as I hear,
Know what I know,
All of who you are in Me.

Walk In My Light!
Let your countenance glow with My Glory.
(Keat Wade 03/15/08)

A Word Fitly Spoken

May our basket be filled
With golden apples of Your word
That we may, in turn, speak
Words fitly spoken and add to other baskets.

Let only the words from You
Become apples of gold
For those to whom
You direct us to speak.

May Your fruit be sweet both
As we receive it...and
As we translate and speak it via
Our silver basket reservoir.

May Your apples have a double anointing
To us who receive them
And to those whom You
Choose to receive them.

As other baskets are filled
May the possessors, in turn
Share Your apples with
Those You send to them.

Human conduits sharing fruit
Through silver baskets
Supernaturally provided
As reservoirs connecting us all.

(Keat Wade 10/06/08)

A Word Fitly Spoken - Proverbs 25: A word fitly spoken is like apples of gold in settings of silver. (NKJV)

Timely advice is lovely, like golden apples in a silver basket. (NLT)

Words fitly spoken are like golden apples in a silver basket. (Personal paraphrase)

2009

When Life is Full

Fullness of Life
Not premised on position,
Age, or state of being
Rather centered on One who is Life
... Life and fullness merge –
Into a supernatural realm
Where He dwells
Bidding us to enter,
Emptied of anything unlike Him.

It is called the state of His Presence –
That place of the serene,
The placid, the secure,
Occupied only by those
Of divine appointment
Preparing a covering mantle
Of Love, Joy, Peace,
An infusion for Longsuffering,
Kindness, and Goodness,
Washed in Faithfulness,
Gentleness, and Self-control
Where we all may know Him
And the Glory
Of entering His dwelling place,
Never leaving it,
For once experienced
Is bonded into our spirit

Anointing the forever footsteps
Of the carriers of His Presence . . .
As life becomes Full

(Keat Wade 01/30/09)

When Life is Full - Acts 2:28 You have made known to me the ways of life; You will make me full of joy in Your presence.

Inverted Hourglass

Move quickly as the first grains of sand
Begin their downward flow
Marking the beginning of
The Kingdom Age.

No time to dwell
Upon the last few grains of the last Age
As we are thrust forward into new realms.

Prepared, equipped, without baggage,
In Kingdom Authority
We must move in instant obedience
Allowing the flow . . .

Light being shattered through
Liquid crystal
Broken into a spectrum
Of hues of blue and indigo
Flashing in sync with
A distinct hue, uniquely ours,
Accompanied by
An emanating, undulating sound that
Comes from deep within
The core of our being
Breaking barriers and strongholds
Formerly unseen, now exposing
Fleeing occupants
Who cannot withstand
The overpowering, penetrating hue of light
And the thundering, shattering sound.

Kingdom of darkness be on notice
That KINGDOM AGE has begun
Led by a remnant
With Kingdom Power and Authority.

As the spectrum of light, our lights,
Shine brilliantly carried on
The bandwidth of New sounds
From Kingdom Carriers resound
In ever expanding circles
ON AND ON AND ON AND ON and on . . .
(Keat Wade 02/27/09)

2010

In the Spray of the Fountain – As a strategically focused prayer group grew out of Uniting Our Hearts In Prayer we playfully called it the Fountain Group since the Lord was giving assignments that seem to flow fountain-like. As I pondered, the Lord gave me a picture of a digitized symphony synchronized with a series of spouting fountains. He showed me that this is the way we were/are functioning in harmony, yet each with his/her specific part for which we had been prepared.

In the Spray of the Fountain

Hearts united in prayer
Moving as one
Into the fountain
He has prepared.

The cooling mist of his anointing
Settles lightly on faces lifted to Him
In majestic, glorious worship
Expressed in the silence of His presence.

Anxious for fresh movement
Deeper into intimacy
Fountain spouts rise and fall

As mist blends with the wafts of His breath
. . . compelling them to "Be still and know. . .I AM!
(Keat Wade 04/22/10

Cross Over Now!

Be it Jordan or wherever I lead you
Step into, step across, wade or swim
As I provide, however, deep, wide, or difficult.
For I AM your provider, nothing is too difficult
When you walk in obedience, in My Presence,
All stops are out as you hear my trumpet
sounding triumphantly
While dirges are heard by our enemies.
The time is NOW to make the crossing
Moving ever forward paving the way
For the free moving of My Presence
To reveal and expose "evil"
And establish our dominion,
When all the people shout and declare,
"KINGDOM, COME!"
(Keat Wade 04/23/10)

Softly Beating Heart – This sequel to the poem, *The Little Girl Within*, again refers to Pat Bahr's near death story. Hearing her share her brief visit to heaven gave me revelation. As Pat traveled to the far reaches of the universe I was reminded of the DVD presentation of *How Big is Your God?* by Louie Giglio when he presented the understanding of Lamimim and its existence in all of God's created cellular structure.

Softly Beating Heart

How softly beats the heart
Defying stethoscope and ears straining to hear.
No breath can be detected
Leaving only an impression of death, permanency.

All the while, romping with Jesus,
Laughing, frolicking, singing,
Then running to plop in His lap,
No smell of death here, or sense of crushing wheels.

Visiting the universe
Flying by planets
And shooting stars
To later learn their names
And how they got there,
In a corner of His universe.

Peace, joy and understanding
Of the enormity of the one who held her hand,
Then, transferring power into her
To be released as she in turn

Encountered others that needed
That touch of transcendent power.

That which was seen at the outer reaches
of the universe
Was seen in the mark of God, of life,
Lamimim in every cell
Now administered at His pleasure through her hands
As she now once again
Returned to complete her destiny, on Earth.

(Keat Wade 04/29/10)

Red, Runs the Rio – Intercessor participants in Border School learned about the troubled U.S. southern border with Mexico, the drug cartels, violence and human trafficking taking place, especially regarding the women. We had seen a video based on the book, *The Killing Fields: Harvest of Women,* by a Texas reporter Diane Washington Valdez, an expose on human trafficking. After hearing her speak, this word picture was painted as a result.

RED, RUNS THE RIO

Corruptions south of our border
Breeds violence, crime, and loss of
many precious lives
Via drug trafficking, territorial control conflict
And . . . then there are the women . . . most
innocent of all.

Trafficked on both sides,
Cheap labor sweatshops,
Brothel babes
Forced servitude
Gifts for favor
They suffer on
Into an uncertain end
Where only death brings peace.

For many, end comes early
When services are no longer
Needed or desired.
However it comes,

Murder is the verdict
With no court or law to uphold it.

They will not be forgotten
Among the desert shrubs
For written forever in the sand beneath them
Are the DNA signatures of each one
Crying out for justice
For the other innocents,
Who will also walk the sidewalks
And dusty paths they trod,
Victims no more,
Free to find their proper destiny.

The border is only a shallow river
Or a dry wash
Whether flowing with water
Or empty . . .
The river continues to run
Crisscrossed with human trafficking
that until it is stopped . . .

RED, RUNS THE RIO!
(Keat Wade 05/01/10)

Voices – The need to learn to distinguish the Lord's voice from all distracting counterfeits became the heart of this writing.

Voices

Subtle at first, even soothing
Was the voice which said,
"Taste and see that it is good. . ."
But the perplexing voice suggested shadows
rather than light.

I was weak . . .

Now, a voice, with clarity and quiet authority
Began to override the shadows
As pure light dissipated the shadows
Allowing truth to emerge and right, prevail.

I was strengthened . . .

The voices intensified, one harsh,
The other, calm, firm, steady, enveloping,
Convincing, exposing deception,
Establishing righteousness and authority.

We overcome in His Presence. . .
(Keat Wade, 05/02/10)

Is That You, God?

Psalm 46:10
Be still, and know that I am God.

Be still

And

Know

That

I

AM

God.

That

Is

All

You

Need

To

Know.

Be

Who

You

Are

And

Allow

Me

To

Be

Who
I

AM.

(Keat Wade 05/25/10)

When Worlds Collide

Caught in the storm
when worlds collide
In the final second heaven battle,
We gather below, sheltered from the fallout,
Under the shadow of His wings
Guided by the light of His countenance
As our fountains flow freely with wisdom waters.
(Keat Wade 07/30/10)

Fountain Covenant – I heard Holy Spirit say, "This is the only poem that we will write with a new stanza coming each day for eight days." There are words like swirling that are used throughout the verses in reference to angels. The reader should get that sense when encountering the words . . . angels?

Fountain Covenant

At the gate called water, they gathered,
To agree together, in covenant as one,
To honor God and one another,
In binding relationship
To serve and carry out
The desires and commands of the supreme
covenanter.

Not blindly, but often
With little understanding,
They act in obedience
To new and unexpected assignments,
To later gain understanding
To serve and carry out
The desires and commands of the supreme
covenanter.
(Keat Wade, 07/22/10)

Following paths once traversed with evil intent
They sought favor to redeem that which
Was intended to defile and corrupt the land
While destroying its occupants and

their freedom gift;
Fountain flowing in the face of the enemy
reclaiming for restoration
That which founding fathers had established.
(added 07/23/10)

Facing desperate new strategies
Flashing out from the chaotic enemy camp
In unmistakable streaks of unconstrained
moral decadence
That tries the souls of a covenant remnant
people crying out
A rallying call heard with final great intensity,
"*'En Punto'* charge forward, there is no retreat!!"
(added 07/28/10)

Caught in the storm when worlds collide
In this second heaven battle,
We gather below, sheltered from the fallout,
Under the shadow of His wings
Guided by the light of His countenance
As our fountains flow freely with wisdom waters.
(added 07/30/10)

It began with a mere waft felt lightly on the cheek
Fluttering into the light breeze of
their passing garments
Stirring stronger, swirling, surrounding, engulfing
In gale force winds of His Spirit, comforting,
Lifting, carrying around, above and through
The garden of the Fountain Keepers.
(added 07/30/10)

Tend your garden well, as you have,
For now I am supplying new seed
That you may sow in your newly turned soil,
Plants of edification, consecration, and dedication
That will yield fruit beyond imagination
Igniting the power placed within you.
(added 07/31/10)

Be steady in the small things,
For they are not as small as they seem.
I have great plans for the accumulating small things
That are being carried out as a part of my
Master Plan.
For the outcomes I have promised
Will fulfill my constant covenant bringing
heaven to earth.

And they will become one as We are and
will be. . .as ONE!
(completed 08/1/10)

Cascading Waterfalls

A day is coming, maybe soon when
The Watergates on the edge of heaven
Will open allowing cascading waters
To flow downward through the battle fields
Of darkness and light, purging the darkness
Unable to longer stand in the sweeping, surging,
Cascading falls from heavenly sources,
Of the purist waters never before felt or tasted,
Eroding and eliminating the battle ground
Washing away the evil combatants
Allowing heaven to settle on earth
Completing His perfect plan
For peace on earth, as it is in heaven,
Now one, an eternal oasis of His love.

(Keat Wade, 08/01/10)

Bombshell – He just gave me a title. Asking, "What do I do with that?" it exploded in my mind and the poem flowed onto the page.

Bombshell

Bursting in air,
giving light, or
on the ground,
clearing the way.

Launched from
Heavenly realms
High above the fray
They come to

Usher in the glory
Of the one
Who is the GLORY
To establish

Permanent residence
Among those who
Have waited,
Believing, with patience

Remnant now fulfilled
In covenant completed,
Trials done
Moving serenely in

The never ending
Forever Light of His Glory

Through the endless
Yet to be seen marvels
Of The creative hand
Extended over and through
The unlimited expanse
Of heaven, engulfing earth,
Our New Home.

(Keat Wade 08/16/10)

Wind and Fire -Then he was told, "Go, stand on the mountain at attention before God. God will pass by." A hurricane wind ripped through the mountains and shattered the rocks before God, but God wasn't to be found in the wind; after the wind an earthquake, but God wasn't in the earthquake; and after the earthquake fire, but God wasn't in the fire; and after the fire a gentle and quiet whisper. I Kings 19:11 (The Message)

Wind and Fire

Though My fire is placed within you,
fanned by the wind of My movement,
let your words be wisely tempered,
uttered gently, yet, with powerful bold authority.
For they are not your words, but Mine,
recognized even by those who deny who I AM
and the authority by which you speak
under the anointing of the King of Kings.

As My leader, remember
When the winds subside,
and fires cool,
Emotions diminish,
and all seems lost,
hear the voice of I AM, saying
"NOW HEAR THIS"
as His servant speaks,
sometimes in strong winds,
other times through the fire,

> but in it all, hear My quiet voice
> meant for you. . .
>   (Keat Wade 08/27/10)

The Black Hole of Despair

You need not go there
Into that black-hole of despair
For your heavenly father
Would never send you there.

But there is one who whispers
Fondly in your ear
Lying and deceiving
Then, abandoning you to fear.

Tune in dear heart.
With frequencies finely tuned
To sort among the voices with clarity,
As not to be consumed.

Allow Him to sort you out
Because you have known His voice
Turning you to the brightness
Of white stairways of His choice.
(Keat Wade 10/12/10)

The Black Hole of Despair - "Oh give thanks to the
Lord, for He is good,
For His mercy endures forever." Ps 136:1

Walk the Path Alone

Confidence, not in myself but Him,
No fear, knowing He is near.
This path less often traveled
We walk alone.

Trusting him for each cautious step
Leading to destinations unknown
But by Him
As we walk the path alone.

His is to know
Ours is to obey
With confidence
And trust, we walk on, alone.

Walking alone with God
Is never a lonely place
Nor is the wilderness of our path
Winding along the desert stream
Of His making
As we walk that path . . . alone?

(Keat Wade 10/17/10)

The Faith Whisperer – If we listen, He overcomes the distracting sounds

The Faith Whisperer

"White noise" that seemed so innocent
Has been exposed
As revelation brings understanding
Of the softly floating voice
That penetrates the deception
In soft whispers sent and received in love.

The voice of the faith whisperer,
Coming from heavenly realms
Far above the fray brings clarity
To deceiving chatter meant to distract and distort,
Flows through the shrouded mist
As light that dispels all darkness.

This whisperer, with soft clarity,
Speaks truth that dissipates
That shrouded mist
Shedding light from the one
Who is light,
As the faith whisperer.
(Keat Wade 10/30/10)

The Dawning of a New Day

Dawn on an Awakening nation
Plagued by enemy deception
From both within and without
Now hearing brave new voices
Laced with truth
From our only true source, Heavenly Father.

Dispelled darkness flees
As light radiates
From the very being of Yeshua
Now astride His white stallion
Sword and trumpet in hand
Prepared to establish His remnant.

No electric horsemen this
For this light is from within,
A continuous supernatural source
Which is the light of the world
And the inner illumination
Of His loyal remnant devotees.

While many will be blinded by it
Because they continue to follow
False lights from the pit of darkness.
Yet, the children of light
Will be drawn to His light
That sets us aglow.

Moving His selected ones
Into positions of authority

By those prepared by Him
From inception
For such a time
As this.

Trust Me
And see
What I will do
As you continue
In worship and prayer
Humbly submitted.

My word is true
And shall be fulfilled
As my remnant people
Wait upon Me
With patience
For My time has no limits.

"Be prepared
For amazing events
That you
Could not have imagined
A short time ago.
Triumph is mine," says the Lord.
(Keat Wade 11/01/10).

Softly the SOUND That THUNDERS

From deep within
Comes a note from the depths
Of my being planted there
As seeds of creation, merged.
A single note that has circled within my being
From its forming
Circling, rising toward a crescendo
Heard by Him, prepared to penetrate hearts.

Shepherding that sound, carefully
As a precious gift
To be used for purposes
Beyond feeble imagination.
Not only from words
But from every gift
Exercised in His name
In forms planted in a poetic heart.

Curling, swirling, wafting, rising,
Invading atmospheres turned
By sensitive hearts and tender spirits
Prepared to receive
That which is meant
To convey poignant messages
From His heart
To needy, receptive souls.

Received as a still small sound
Or a thundering crescendo
Enlightening, encouraging,

Prophesying words,
Hearts are stirred
Into mind, body or spirit
Action that becomes
Its own answer for that requested.

Not a planned sound
But one that comes
From deep within
As the times with Him.
In His presence,
Spontaneously erupting
As an unsolicited sound
From beyond known depths and imagination.
Never silent,
Only quiet to the undiscerning ear
Often drowned out by the babblers
Of the noisome pestilent
Who, for the lack of knowledge
Fall prey to their own distractions;
Yet, heard by the tender spirit
Of those who know the truly-tuned sound.

Release the sound within you
That it may reach out across through
Empty expanses, to mingle such sounds
Coming together creating
A symphony for the Lord
To enhance new atmospheres
Where His Spirit can flourish
In a thundering crescendo of blessing.
(Keat Wade 11/08/10)

The Power of Alignment

Vertical from Him
Then flowing horizontally
Among us, that which
Brings complete alignment.

When we come into alignment
Verticality with His purpose
The flow increases through us
Into a horizontal flooding stream.

We cannot allow
That which would break
Or stem the flow
And deny pure waters from above.

Only stagnation
And shrinking pools
Result when we lean, ever slightly
From the 90^0 vertical,

Let not the flow stop here, Lord.
I will stay in the vertical
With you
That the power of alignment may be seen.
(Keat Wade 11/08/10)

Be Still and Know That I AM. . . Will

Pray with bold assurance
Believing Me for My Word
Spoken to you
Knowing that I AM, will.

My Word not idly given
Nor casually written Stands,
As for centuries as eternal TRUTH
Then, now, and forever more.

Be still and know that I AM. . . WILL
Prevail,
Lead,
Conquer,
Restore,
Establish
Heaven
On
Earth
As
Our
Shared
Home
With
I AM.

(Keat Wade 11/09/10)

"MARCH!"

Do you feel the sound
in response to the command;
marching, treading, marching,
on and on reclaiming old territory
and claiming anew
what is rightfully ours?

Hut two three four
do you feel the rhythm
or hear the cadence count
ringing o'er the land?
The army of the Lord is building,
moving rank upon rank.

The army grows as it moves
from the Pacific shores
flooding over mountains
flowing through valleys
spreading outward as it
swells the resonance of pounding feet.

Nothing is exempt in its mighty path
reaching ever eastward, combining
forces along the way, soon to cover
a nation from sea to shining sea
Pacific to Atlantic, Gulf of Mexico
to Canadian Provinces, all inclusive.

Man's boundaries will not deter
as the Army sweeps south reclaiming

and redeeming Ancient Latin lands
while marching, treading northward
into lands thawing under
the heat and spirit of so vast an Army.

Lands are being restored
by spiritual weapons
that have always been there
only now being realized
for the power they possess
which cannot be resisted.

God's Army is moving on
marching, treading, marching,
reclaiming, restoring, redeeming
that which was taken away
now, ever under His control.
Do you feel the sound?
(Keat Wade 11/12/10)

Our Hearing Hearts

No voice came clear
Through the wind, earthquake and fire,
Until. Oh so clear, a still small voice,
Detected only by a hearing heart
On Horeb where the servant of the most high
Covered his face, his fear allayed.

Using our gifts to observe, perceive and discern
through seeing souls
And hearing hearts, we know
That I AM has spoken
And sends his accompanying
Angels as escorts on our assigned journey.

Now, we must release Your sound
To go forth with new Words
Conveyed through
New covenantal authority
Via proclamations and knowledge
From divine authority.

(Keat Wade 11/19/10)

Time Traveler - Then and Now

Through this lifetime,
a mere instant in time, His time,
incident by incident
yet, an instant panorama
now seen as climatic, building
toward a yet unseen fulfillment.

Left to wild, vivid imaginations
of lonely childhood,
a developing sense
of service and meaningful contribution,
coupled with divinely directed
peculiar interests, came late, but productive focus.

Now, experiencing the flow of Holy Spirit words
Downloaded directly through
His SpiritedPen, now in the hand
Of His designated writer
Words of prophetic inspiration
Appearing on the screen, meant for each receiver's
heart.

. . . that if there is any virtue or anything
in such words, you may meditate on them
that He may be your Peace.

(Keat Wade 11/26/10)

Three Angel Poems – Written on my Blackberry while waiting on "Stand-by" all day for a flight out of the San Diego airport.

Three Angel Poems

The Sound of Angels

Through my hearing heart
Do I detect the otherwise
Indiscernible vibrations
From a time and dimension
Yet parallel to the one
Of our existence, linked eternally?

[Keat Wade 12/04/10]

Quiet Assurance

Unseen and unheard
Yet, with quiet assurance,
Moving among us,
They bring safety and peace
Under powerful spiritual wings
Folding us in tender arms.

[Keat Wade 12/04/10]

In the Quiet of the Stillness

With nighttime stillness comes
Sweet sleep, while hovering
In the quiet, faithful protectors

Continue their watchful care.
We are His and they are ours.

(Keat Wade 12/04/10)

From the Courtroom of Heaven

From the courtroom of heaven
The gavel comes down
And the sound reverberates
Throughout the universe,
Setting our spirits in motion,
Coming into alignment
With that of His court.

Prepared, now, to transition
Into our new realm-level assignments,
Vibrating with fresh on-high strength
Walking boldly erect, penetrating
Beachheads, as arrows of flint,
Weakening enemy strongholds,
Preparing a way for His Conquering bands,
Prepared to recover that which was stolen. . . and
STAND!!

(Keat Wade 12/09/10)

Bushes and Bulrushes

Out of the river to face the fire
Of a burning bush that could not be consumed
Became an assigned journey for a man
With only a robe and a rod
Called to return, stand firm,
Speak the Word for the Lord and deliver a people.
(Keat Wade 12/27/10)

2011

Shabbat Shalom

Gather in My name
That My Peace
May pervade your atmosphere
And fill your being.

Tap into Me,
Tribe by tribe,
That you may rise
And move with Me
In a time and dimension
That you have not known,
As you learn more of I AM
For seasons ahead
That understanding "As One" becomes yours.

(Keat Wade 01/07/11)

Oh, Little Town of Escondido – This poem came after we returned from a prayer initiative.

Oh, Little Town of Escondido

From a strange, hidden garden reflecting darkness
In its mirrored expanse,
Has become a place of birthing
Of that which will consume it,
Converting it, restoring its land
Through redemption for future generations
Beginning now and for eternity.

Your places dedicated to darkness
Shall become a center for cultivated gardens
Of divine beauty and provision
Shining forth with purity and
Peace beyond understanding
Plain to see in un-mirrored brilliance
Which will not be dimmed or diminished.

The tide has already turned
In the battle between heaven and earth
Which has raged over you.
"It is mine," says God of-the-Angel-Armies
For I am posting my appointed ones
At your portal gates as My encroaching army
Encamps round about, entering to establish My rule.

KINGDOM COME, MY WILL BE DONE!
(Keat Wade 01/08/11)

Enter Intercession, California – A poem prayer-call to intercessors for California.

Enter Intercession, California

Join the voices of your remnant people
Who have been crying out to Me
Oh of sad misnomer
Release your voice that has, for so long
Been suppressed, subdued into silence,
That the promised turning may come
Only as it comes from within the depths
Of your canyon faults, no longer
Spewing death and destruction.

But, now crying out in humble songs of repentance
Singing not siren songs, but rather
Songs of turning to the author of cleansing streams
And healing waters purging your tainted land
Calming the turmoil of bloodied conflicts of greed
and self-seeking.

Speak faith, hope, and love into your land, recorded
in your stones,
As I spoke it into my people, to be remembered in
reverberated sound
Through ages to come that you may be preserved
As the "ring of fire" cools, allowing the birthing of
My government
To reign and rule, bringing eternal light and peace
over your lands

That they may be a shelter, provider and haven for all who hear
... the song of my voice crying from the stones of My wilderness, New California.

(Keat Wade 01/16/11)

Beasts and Angels

Roaming the earth
Ready to devour
Yet, unaware of powerful bodies,
Racing above, poised to pounce
At the impulse received from
Eyes of unrestricted, unlimited vision.

The battle is on, now on the offensive,
The God-of-the-angel-armies readily dispatches
Rank upon rank, squadron upon squadron
Upon the free-reigning beasts of the enemy
To be reined in, stripped of power and authority
Rendered useless against forces never anticipated or
seen.

The time has come in the now of this day
For the army of the Lord to consume the enemy
Taking back the ground once forfeited
To be redeemed, regained, and ruled
By the remnant heirs now in place
... to move in lockstep angel rhythm.

(Keat Wade 01/20/11)

Cherishing the Secret Place - All about seeking and finding intimacy with the Father.

Cherishing the Secret Place

Where I come to You
And You come to me
Is our secret place
Of closed doors and open heavens.

A place of open speaking
And secret seeing.
Where honesty in His presence
Has its own rewards.

A place of anointing,
Washed clean
Of false appearances
In Your sight.

A pavilion, a tabernacle
Of hiding, a place upon a high rock
Deep within Your presence
Of strife-free speaking.

When my troubled call was heard
You came and delivered me
Thundering Your answer
Keeping me in Your comforting cloak of silence.

Nothing wanting in that place
With gushing waters like those of Meribah
Satisfying, and cleansing
Those who take shelter In the Secret Place

. . . . . All under the shadow of the Almighty.
(Keat Wade 01/23/11)

Chosen and Prepared

Selected vessel
Sixty-six years in preparation,
Twelve years in gestation
Now ready to give birth.

A chronology of love
Through
SpiritedPen
Now a living, breathing life form
Destined for stimulated
Growth in the soul of the reader.

(Keat Wade 02/08/11)

When you look at yesterday through the eyes of today you will see that tomorrow held much more promise than you were seeing through the eyes of today. Enjoy today for it's own promise and be reminded that yesterday's eyes for today are today's eyes for tomorrow. Then, remember that God sees and knows all our tomorrows. They are His. You know that He is the same yesterday, today and forever (tomorrow). Trust Him with all your tomorrows by walking in faith and obedience in all your todays! Now your trust level will cause the pain of your yesterdays to fade in the light of today and tomorrow's promise.

Afterword

Bushes and Bulrushes

Out of the river to face the fire
Of a burning bush that could not be consumed
Became an assigned journey for a man
With only a robe and a rod
Called to return, stand firm,
Speak the Word for the Lord and deliver a people.
(Keat Wade 12/27/10)

APPENDIX

Alphabetical Listing of Poems

A Word Fitly Spoken	10/06/08
Acknowledged By Him	04/12/06
Across the Fire	09/20/05
And the Waters Shall Flow	03/21/04
As the Sound of Many Waters	03/25/06
Awash with His Sound	09/23/05
Be Still	08/15/05
Be Still and Know That I AM . . . Will	11/09/10
Beasts and Angels	01/20/11
Becoming the NOW	01/20/06
Behold the Days	10/21/05
Birth of the SpiritedPen	08/03/02
Black Hole of Despair, The	10/12/10
Bombshell	08/16/10

Breaking of the Dawn   11/21/04
Breath of God – Breath of Life   01/11/02
Bushes and Bulrushes   12/27/10
By His Light   01/01/01
Can You Hear Our Mountain Sing?   03/27/04
Cascading Waterfalls   08/01/10
Cherishing the Secret Place   01/23/11
Chosen and Prepared   02/08/11
Circles   01/01/01
Cloud and the Glory, The   09/10/02
Cross Over, Now   04/23/10
Dawning of a New Day, The   11/01/10
Do You Hear It a Rumblin'   01/26/03
Enter Intercession California   01/16/11
Eternal Glimpses   01/13/05
Faith Whisperer   10/30/10
Faithful Housewives   04/05/06
Flowing Into His River   08/29/02
Forever   09/10/02
Fountain Covenant   08/01/10
From the Courtroom of Heaven   12/09/10
Go for the Gold   04/01/06
Harp and Bowl, Heaven and Earth   01/26/03
Connectors
He Cometh   01/30/06
He Gave Me a Golden Scepter   01/27/03
He Is Our Peace   08/10/05

His Name	01/26/03
His Voice	07/21/02
Hope Deferred	02/03/04
House Within, The	07/13/03
I Am the Land	03/14/04
If This Land Could Speak	02/17/05
In Anticipation	01/07/99
In the Golden Glow of His Glory	10/24/04
In the Spray of the Fountain	04/22/10
In This Place	10/10/04
Increase My Desire	03/31/02
Inverted Hourglass	02/27/09
Is That You, God?	05/25/10
It Happens At the Cross	03/27/05
It Is Coming	01/27/04
It's Time Has Come	04/01/03
Light of His Countenance, The	11/28/01
Lighthouses and Foghorns	02/04/03
Like No Other	08/12/07
Little Girl Within	05/03/05
Love Banner	03/26/02
Love Worth Living	10/12/99
Majesty On the Mountain	08/22/99
March	11/12/10
Master Pilot's Call, The	12/01/02
Mute Before the Throne	11/16/05
My Praise, They Shall Declare	02/08/05

New Sound, The   07/27/05
Ode to My Sandcastle   09/10/01
Oh Little Town of Escondido   01/08/11
On My Heart, Lord   08/24/02
On the Wings of Your Wind   09/17/06
On Wings As Eagles   08/06/03
Once Upon a Century   03/28/02
Our Hearing Hearts   11/19/10
Out of the Cave   03/27/04
Overwhelmed   05/12/05
Pegs for the Lord   04/11/02
Power, The   08/24/02
Power of Alignment   11/08/10
Power of Silence, The   06/12/05
Praise. . .   01/24/02
Pressing On   01/21/01
Provision   01/21/03
Quakes, Shakes, & Other Phenomenon   09/09/05
Read the Wind   03/07/04
Red, Runs the Rio   05/01/10
Safe Harbor   11/24/99
Seasons of Remembrance   08/24/02
Shabbat Shalom   01/07/11
Silence, The   07/02/05
Softly Beating Heart   04/29/10
Softly the SOUND That THUNDERS   11/08/10
Spirit of Interfaith   02/03/03

Spiritual Presidios	08/25/02
Submission In the Shadow of His Hand	07/21/02
Symphony from His Heart	11/03/04
Three Angel Poems	12/04/10
Time Traveler – Then and Now	11/26/10
Upon This Mountain	06/01/02
Vision from Michelangelo	12/08/07
Voice of the Shofar, The	05/17/02
Voices	05/02/10
Walk In His Light	03/15/08
Walk of Love	02/13/06
Walk the Path Alone	10/17/10
Walking Words	08/14/07
Watch and See	01/14/03
Watch for the Fire	11/19/02
What Have I to Fear?	01/01/03
When I Choose The Proper Time	07/16/02
When Life Is Full	01/30/09
When Silence Thunders	11/08/07
When World's Collide	07/30/10
Where the Spirit Flows	04/12/03
Wilderness of His Love	07/11/03
Wilderness Unto Wilderness	02/08/05
Wings of the Dawn	04/01/04
Wind and Fire	08/27/10
Within the Depths	11/21/05
Wonder of Bonnie Brae	03/10/05

Wonder of Wonders   01/25/03
Worship, the Mantle of His Glory   05/10/02
Your Living Word   08/24/99

CPSIA information can be obtained at www.ICGtesting.com
Printed in the USA
LVOW041356170112

264275LV00001B/2/P